300
FANTASTIC FACTS

EARTH

300 FANTASTIC FACTS

EARTH

Written by: Clare Oliver, Peter Riley

Miles Kelly

First published in 2016 by Miles Kelly Publishing Ltd
Harding's Barn, Bardfield End Green, Thaxted, Essex, CM6 3PX, UK

2 4 6 8 10 9 7 5 3 1

Publishing Director Belinda Gallagher
Creative Director Jo Cowan
Editorial Director Rosie Neave
Designers John Christopher (White Design), Rob Hale, Venita Kidwai
Cover Designer Rob Hale
Image Manager Liberty Newton
Production Elizabeth Collins, Caroline Kelly
Reprographics Stephan Davis, Jennifer Barker, Thom Allaway
Consultants Clive Carpenter, Clint Twist

ISBN 978-1-78209-764-8

Printed in China

British Library Cataloguing-in-Publication Data
A catalogue record for this book is available from the British Library

Made with paper from a sustainable forest

www.mileskelly.net
info@mileskelly.net

Contents

1 The Earth is a huge ball of rock moving through space at nearly 3000 metres per second. It weighs 6000 million, million, million tonnes. Up to two-thirds of the Earth's rocky surface is covered by water – this makes up the seas and oceans. Rock that is not covered by water makes up the land. Surrounding the Earth is a layer of gases called the atmosphere (air). This reaches to about 1000 kilometres above the Earth's surface – then space begins.

▶ Earth and the planets nearest to it in the Solar System. Mercury, the planet closest to the Sun, is small and hot. Venus and Earth are rocky and cooler.

VENUS

MERCURY

SUN

MOON

EARTH

Where did Earth come from?

2 **The Earth came from a cloud in space.** Scientists think it formed from a huge cloud of gas and dust around 4500 million years ago. A star near the cloud exploded, making the cloud spin. As the cloud span, gases gathered at its centre and formed the Sun. Dust whizzed around the Sun and began to stick together to form lumps of rock. In time, the rocks crashed into each other and made the planets. The Earth is one of these planets.

▶ Clouds of gas and dust are made from the remains of old stars that have exploded or run out of energy. It is from these clouds that new stars and planets form.

⑤ The Earth was made up of one large piece of land, now split into seven chunks known as continents

① Cloud starts to spin

④ Volcanoes erupt, releasing gases, helping to form the early atmosphere

③ The Earth begins to cool and a hard shell forms

② Dust gathers into lumps of rock that form a small planet

3 **At first the Earth was very hot.** As the rocks collided they heated each other up. Later, as the Earth formed, the rocks inside it melted. The new Earth was a ball of liquid rock with a thin, solid shell.

4 Huge numbers of large rocks called meteorites crashed into the Earth. They made round hollows on the surface. These hollows are called craters. The Moon was hit with meteorites at the same time. Look at the Moon with binoculars – you can see the craters that were made long ago.

▶ The Moon was hit by meteorites, which made huge craters and mountain ranges up to 5000 metres high.

▼ Erupting volcanoes and fierce storms helped form the atmosphere and oceans. These provided energy that was needed for life on Earth to begin.

5 The seas and oceans formed as the Earth cooled down. Volcanoes erupted, letting out steam, gases and rocks. As the Earth cooled, the steam changed to water droplets and formed clouds. As the Earth cooled further, rain fell from the clouds. It took millions of years of rain to form the seas and oceans.

I DON'T BELIEVE IT!
Millions of rocks crash into Earth as it speeds through space. Some larger ones may reach the ground as meteorites.

In a spin

6 The Earth is like a spinning top. It continues to spin because it was formed from a spinning cloud of gas and dust. The Earth turns around an invisible line called an axis. It does not spin straight up but leans to one side. The Earth takes 24 hours to spin around once – we call this period of time a day.

▲ As one half of the Earth turns towards sunlight, the other half turns towards darkness. It is morning when one half turns into sunlight, and evening as the other half turns into darkness.

7 Spinning makes day and night. Each part of the Earth spins towards the Sun, and then away from it every day. When a part of the Earth is facing the Sun it is daytime there. When that part is facing away from the Sun it is nighttime. Is the Earth facing the Sun or facing away from it where you are?

8 The Earth spins around two points on its surface. They are at opposite ends of the planet. One is at the top of the Earth, called the North Pole. The other is at the bottom of the Earth. It is called the South Pole. The North and South Poles are covered by ice and snow all year round.

9 The spinning Earth acts like a magnet. At the centre of the Earth is liquid iron. As the Earth spins, it makes the iron behave like a magnet with a North and South Pole. These act on the magnet in a compass to make the needle point to the North and South Poles.

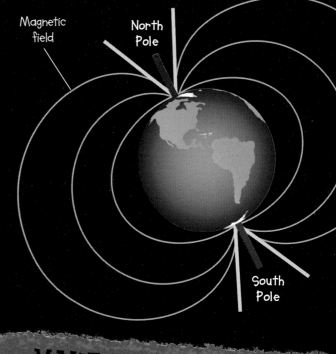

North Pole

▼ If you were in space and looked at the Earth from the side, it would appear to move from left to right. If you looked down on Earth from the North Pole, it would seem to be moving anticlockwise.

▼ These lines show the pulling power of the magnet inside the Earth.

Magnetic field

North Pole

Direction of Earth's spin

South Pole

Axis

South Pole

▲ The region around the North Pole is called the Arctic. It consists of the Arctic Ocean, which is mainly covered in a layer of floating ice.

MAKE A COMPASS

You will need:
bowl of water   piece of wood
bar magnet   real compass

Place the wood in the water with the magnet on top. Make sure they do not touch the sides. When the wood is still, check which way the magnet is pointing with your compass, by placing it on a flat surface. It will tell you the direction of the Poles.

Inside the Earth

10 There are different layers inside the Earth. There is a thin, rocky crust on the surface, a solid middle called the mantle and a centre called the core. The outer core is liquid but the inner part of the core is solid metal.

11 At the centre of the Earth is a huge metal ball called the inner core. It is 2500 kilometres wide and is made mainly from iron, with some nickel. The ball has an incredible temperature of around 7000°C – hot enough to make the metals melt. However, they stay solid because the other layers of the Earth push down heavily on them.

12 Around the centre of the Earth flows a hot, liquid layer of iron and nickel. This layer is the outer core and is about 2200 kilometres thick. As the Earth spins, the inner and outer core move at different speeds.

13 The largest layer is called the mantle. It is around 2900 kilometres thick. It lies between the core and the crust. The mantle is made of soft, hot rock. In the upper mantle, near the crust, the rock moves more slowly.

Atmosphere

Crust

Mantle
4500°C

Outer core
5000°C

Inner core
7000°C

◀ The internal structure of the Earth. The centre of the Earth – the inner core – is solid even though it is intensely hot. This is because it is under extreme pressure.

North American plate

Eurasian plate

Pacific plate

Pacific plate

South American plate

African plate

Australian plate

Antarctic plate

▲ Six of the seven tectonic plates carry a continent. The Pacific plate does not.

15 **The crust is divided into huge slabs of rock called tectonic plates.** The plates all have both land and seas on top of them except for the Pacific plate, which is just covered by water. The large areas of land on the plates are called continents. There are seven continents in total – Africa, Asia, Europe, North America, South America, Oceania and Antarctica.

14 **The Earth's surface is covered by crust.** Land is made of continental crust between 20 and 70 kilometres thick. Most of this is made from a rock called granite. The ocean bed is made of oceanic crust about eight kilometres thick. It is made mainly from a rock called basalt.

▼ The Great Rift Valley in Kenya is part of a huge system of rift valleys. It is the result of tectonic plates moving apart, causing the Earth's crust to separate.

16 **Very, very slowly, the continents are moving.** Slow-flowing mantle under the crust moves the tectonic plates across the Earth's surface. As the plates move, so do the continents. In some places, the plates push into each other. In others, they move apart. North America is moving three centimetres away from Europe every year!

Hot rocks

17 There are places on Earth where hot, liquid rocks shoot up through the surface. These are volcanoes. Beneath a volcano is a huge space filled with molten (liquid) rock. This is the magma chamber. Inside the chamber, pressure builds like the pressure in a fizzy drink's can if you shake it. Ash, steam and molten rock called lava escape from the top of the volcano – this is an eruption.

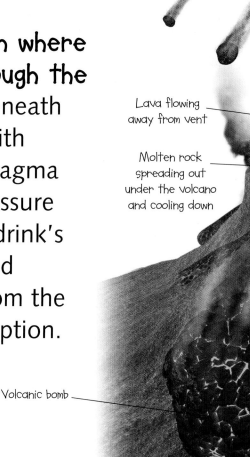

Lava flowing away from vent

Molten rock spreading out under the volcano and cooling down

Volcanic bomb

▶ When a volcano erupts, the hot rock from inside the Earth escapes as ash, smoke, lumps of rock called volcanic bombs and rivers of lava.

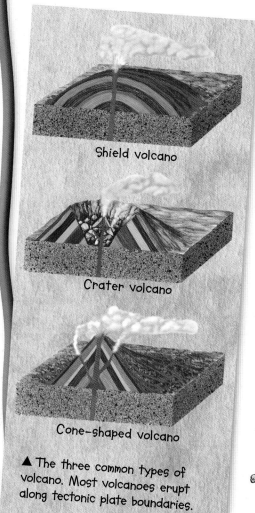

Shield volcano

Crater volcano

Cone-shaped volcano

▲ The three common types of volcano. Most volcanoes erupt along tectonic plate boundaries.

18 Volcanoes erupt in different ways and form different shapes. Most have a central 'pipe', reaching from the magma chamber up to the vent opening. Some volcanoes have runny lava. It flows from the vent and makes a domed shape called a shield volcano. Other volcanoes have thick lava. When they erupt, gases in the lava make it explode into pieces of ash. The ash settles on the lava to make a cone-shaped volcano. A caldera, or crater volcano, is made when the top of a cone-shaped volcano explodes and sinks into the magma chamber.

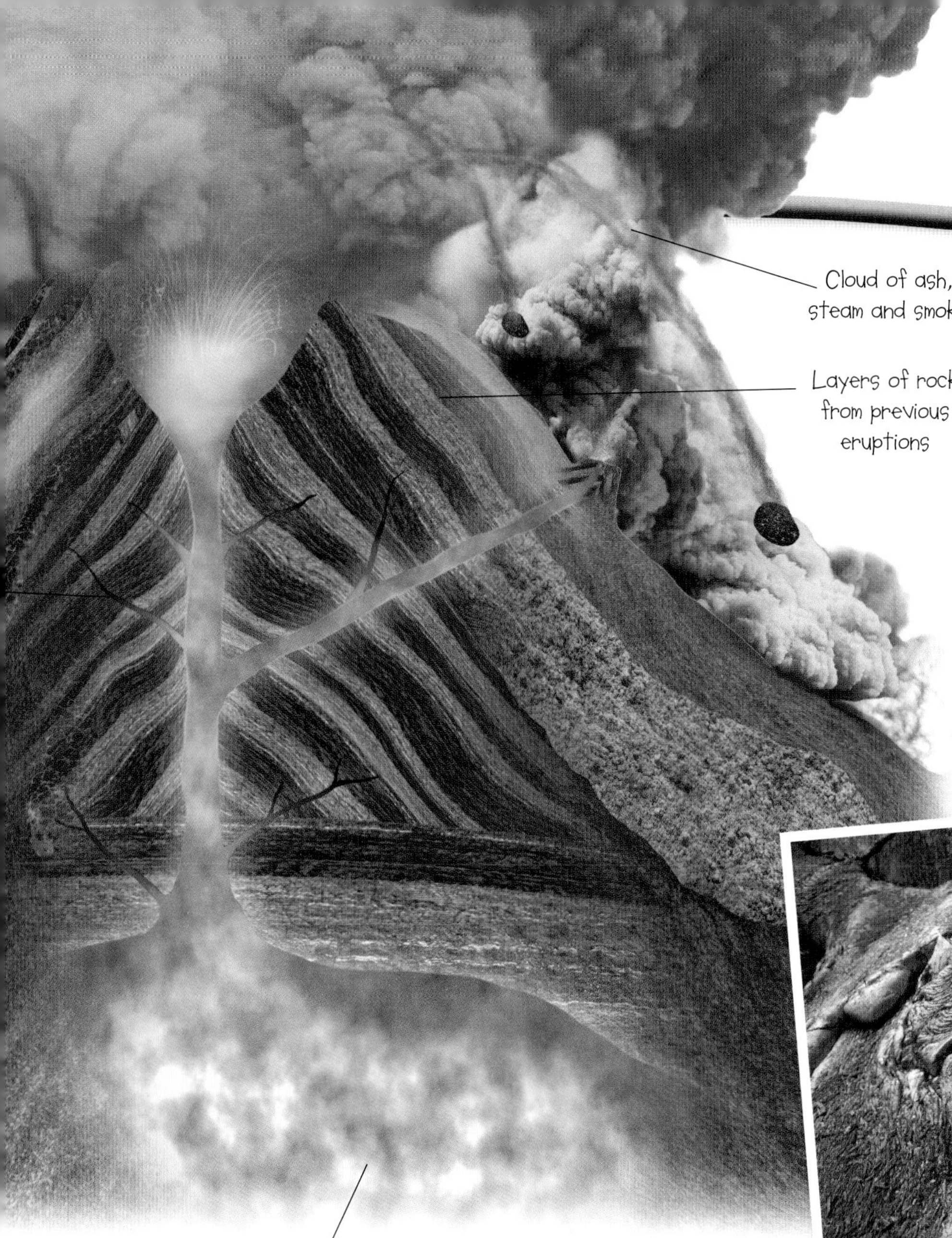

Cloud of ash, steam and smoke

Layers of rock from previous eruptions

19 There are volcanoes under the sea. Where tectonic plates move apart, lava flows out from rift volcanoes to fill the gap. The hot lava is cooled quickly by the sea and forms pillow-shaped lumps called pillow lava.

Huge chamber of magma (molten rock) beneath the volcano

▶ Pillow lava piles up on the coast of Hawaii, following an eruption of the Kilauea volcano.

MAKE A VOLCANO

You will need:
bicarbonate of soda   a plastic bottle
food colouring   vinegar   sand

Put a tablespoon of bicarbonate of soda in the bottle. Stand it in a tray with a cone of sand around it. Put a few drops of red food colouring in half a cup of vinegar. Pour this into the bottle. In a few moments the volcano should erupt with red, frothy lava.

20 Hot rocks don't always reach the surface. Huge lumps of rock can rise into the crust and become stuck. These are batholiths. The rock cools slowly and large crystals form. When the crystals cool, they form a rock called granite. In time, the surface of the crust may wear away and the top of the batholith appears above ground.

Boil and bubble

21 **Geysers can be found above old volcanoes.** If volcanoes collapse, the rocks settle above hot rocks in the magma chamber. The gaps between the broken rocks make pipes and chambers. Rain water collects in the chambers, where it heats until it boils. Steam builds up, pushing the water through the pipes and out of an opening called a nozzle. Steam and water shoot up, making a fountain up to 60 metres high.

MAKE A GEYSER

You will need:
bucket   plastic funnel   plastic tubing

Fill a bucket with water. Turn the plastic funnel upside down and sink most of it in the water. Take a piece of plastic tube and put one end under the funnel. Blow down the other end of the tube. A spray of water and air will shoot out of the funnel. Be prepared for a wet face!

22 **In a hot spring, the water bubbles gently to the surface.** As the water is heated in the chamber, it rises up a pipe and into a pool. The pool may be brightly coloured due to tiny plants and animals called algae and bacteria. These live in large numbers in the hot water.

▶ In Iceland, visitors watch the Strokkur geyser erupt.

Clouds of mineral particles forming black smoke

Giant tube worms

Superheated water

Chimney (stack)

▲ The rocky chimneys of a black smoker are built up over time by minerals in the hot water.

24 Wallowing in a mud pot can make your skin soft. A mud pot is made when fumes from underground break down rocks into tiny pieces. These mix with water to make mud. Hot gases push through the mud, making it bubble. Some mud pots are cool enough to wallow in.

25 Steam and smelly fumes can escape from holes in the ground. These holes are called fumaroles. Since Roman times, people have used the steam from fumaroles for steam baths. The steam may keep joints and lungs healthy.

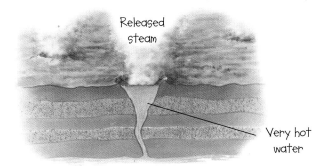

Released steam

Very hot water

▲ Under a fumarole the water gets so hot that it turns to steam, then shoots upwards into the air.

23 Deep in the ocean are hot springs called black smokers. They form near rift volcanoes, where magma is close to the ocean floor. Water seeps into cracks in rocks and is heated. The hot water dissolves minerals from the surrounding rock as it travels upwards. The minerals in the water produce dark clouds that look like smoke.

26 In Iceland, underground steam is used to make lights work. The steam is sent to power stations and is used to work generators to make electricity. The electricity then flows to homes and powers electrical equipment such as lights, televisions and computers.

17

Breaking down rocks

27 Ice has the power to break open rocks. In cold weather, rain water gets into cracks in rocks and freezes. The water expands as it turns to ice. The ice pushes with such power on the rock that it opens up the cracks. Over a long time, a rock can be broken down into thousands of tiny pieces.

▲ Ice has broken through rocks in a creek, forcing the layers apart and breaking off fragments.

28 Living things can break down rocks. Sometimes a tree seed lands in a crack in a rock. In time, a tree grows and its large roots force open the rock. Tiny living things called lichens dissolve the surface of rocks to reach minerals they need to live. When animals, such as rabbits, make a burrow they may break up some of the rock in the ground.

▼ Tree roots grow in joints in many rocks. As the roots get larger, the rock is forced apart.

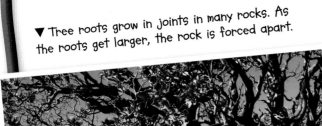

29 Warming up and cooling down can break rocks into flakes. When a rock warms up it swells a little. When it cools, the rock shrinks back to its original size. After swelling and shrinking many times, some rocks break up into flakes. Sometimes layers of large flakes form on a rock, making it look like the skin of an onion.

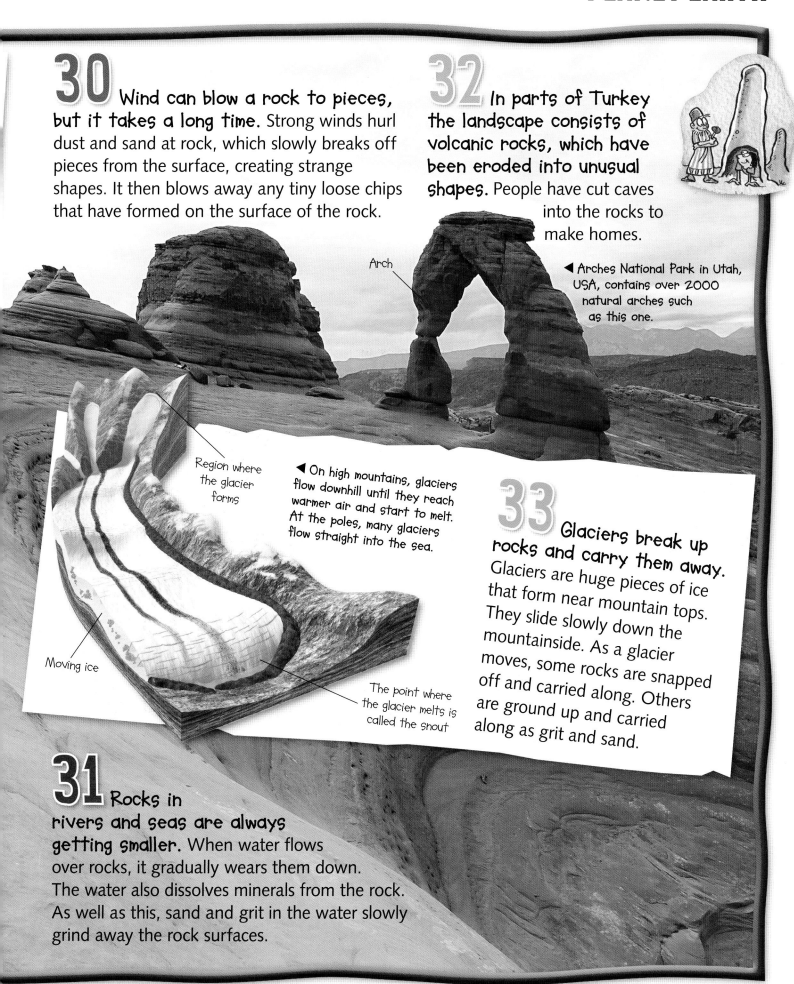

30
Wind can blow a rock to pieces, but it takes a long time. Strong winds hurl dust and sand at rock, which slowly breaks off pieces from the surface, creating strange shapes. It then blows away any tiny loose chips that have formed on the surface of the rock.

32
In parts of Turkey the landscape consists of volcanic rocks, which have been eroded into unusual shapes. People have cut caves into the rocks to make homes.

◄ Arches National Park in Utah, USA, contains over 2000 natural arches such as this one.

Arch

Region where the glacier forms

◄ On high mountains, glaciers flow downhill until they reach warmer air and start to melt. At the poles, many glaciers flow straight into the sea.

Moving ice

The point where the glacier melts is called the snout

33
Glaciers break up rocks and carry them away. Glaciers are huge pieces of ice that form near mountain tops. They slide slowly down the mountainside. As a glacier moves, some rocks are snapped off and carried along. Others are ground up and carried along as grit and sand.

31
Rocks in rivers and seas are always getting smaller. When water flows over rocks, it gradually wears them down. The water also dissolves minerals from the rock. As well as this, sand and grit in the water slowly grind away the rock surfaces.

19

Settling down

34 Stones of different sizes can combine to make rock. Thousands of years ago, boulders, pebbles and gravel settled on the shores of seas and lakes. Over time, these have become stuck together to make a type of rock called conglomerate. At the foot of cliffs, broken, rocky pieces have collected and joined together to make a rock called breccia.

▲ Pieces of rock can become stuck together by a natural cement to make a lump of larger rock, such as breccia.

▼ These chalk cliffs in Dorset, England have been eroded over time to create sea stacks.

35 A form of limestone, chalk is made from millions of shells of tiny sea creatures. A drop of sea water contains many microscopic organisms (living things), some of which have shells. When the organisms die, the shells sink to the seabed and in time form chalk, which builds up to form rocks and cliffs.

36 Limestone is basically the mineral calcite, often with bits from sea creatures, broken into various sizes. There are many types of limestone, depending on what it contains – coralline limestone has remains of corals, shelly limestone has shells, and so on.

▲ Limestone is usually white, cream, grey or yellow. Caves often form in areas of limestone.

37 If mud is squashed hard enough, it turns to stone. Mud is made from tiny particles of clay and slightly larger particles called silt. When huge layers of mud formed in ancient rivers, lakes and seas, they were squashed by their own weight to make mudstone.

▶ Mudstone has a very smooth surface. It may be grey, black, brown or yellow.

38 Sandstone can be made in the sea or in the desert. When a thick layer of sand builds up, the grains are pressed together and cement forms. This sticks the grains together to make sandstone. Sea sandstone may be yellow with sharp-edged grains. Desert sandstone may be red with round, smooth grains.

◀ Sandstone can form impressive shapes. These pillars in Arches National Park, Utah, USA, are known as the Fins.

I DON'T BELIEVE IT!

Flint is found in chalk and limestone. Thousands of years ago people used flint to make axes, knives and arrow heads.

Uncovering fossils

39 Fossils are formed from animals and plants that were buried. When a plant or animal dies, it is usually eaten by other living things so that nothing remains. If the plant or animal was buried quickly after death, or even buried alive, its body may be preserved.

▼ Prehistoric ocean-dwelling creatures, such as this ichthyosaur, are more likely to leave fossils than those on land.

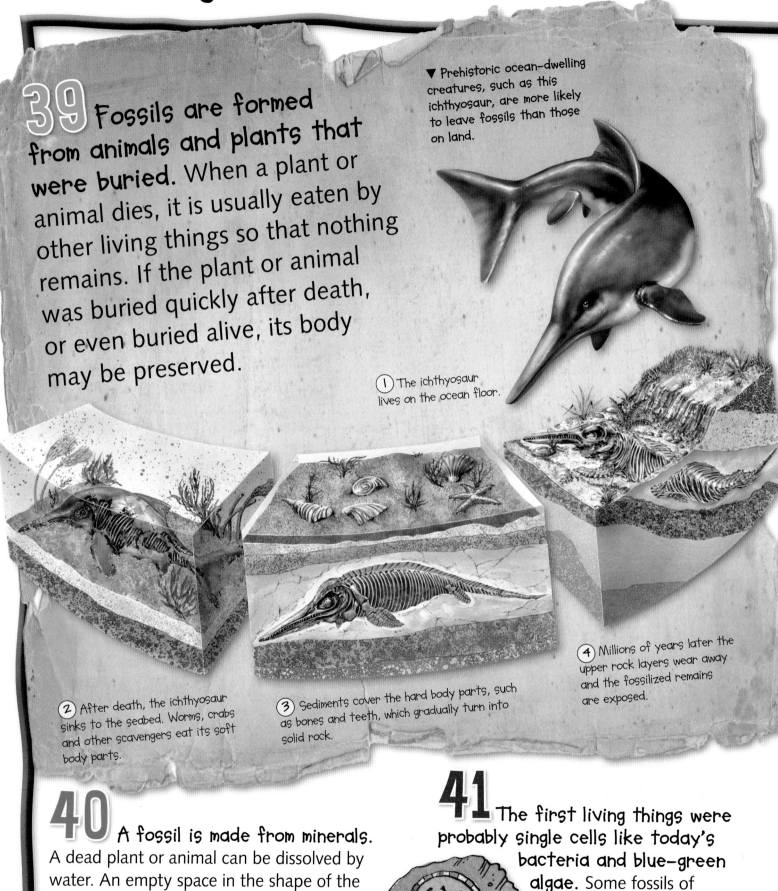

① The ichthyosaur lives on the ocean floor.

② After death, the ichthyosaur sinks to the seabed. Worms, crabs and other scavengers eat its soft body parts.

③ Sediments cover the hard body parts, such as bones and teeth, which gradually turn into solid rock.

④ Millions of years later the upper rock layers wear away and the fossilized remains are exposed.

40 A fossil is made from minerals. A dead plant or animal can be dissolved by water. An empty space in the shape of the plant or animal is left in the mud and fills with minerals from the surrounding rock.

41 The first living things were probably single cells like today's bacteria and blue-green algae. Some fossils of bacteria are three and a half billion years old.

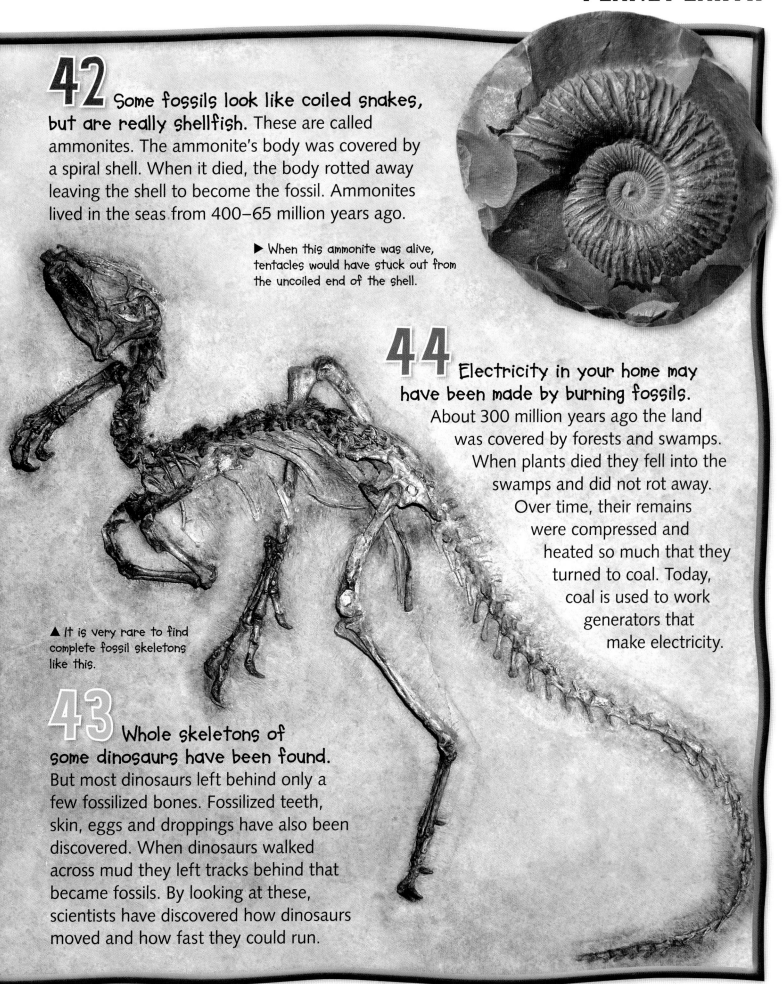

42 Some fossils look like coiled snakes, but are really shellfish. These are called ammonites. The ammonite's body was covered by a spiral shell. When it died, the body rotted away leaving the shell to become the fossil. Ammonites lived in the seas from 400–65 million years ago.

▶ When this ammonite was alive, tentacles would have stuck out from the uncoiled end of the shell.

44 Electricity in your home may have been made by burning fossils. About 300 million years ago the land was covered by forests and swamps. When plants died they fell into the swamps and did not rot away. Over time, their remains were compressed and heated so much that they turned to coal. Today, coal is used to work generators that make electricity.

▲ It is very rare to find complete fossil skeletons like this.

43 Whole skeletons of some dinosaurs have been found. But most dinosaurs left behind only a few fossilized bones. Fossilized teeth, skin, eggs and droppings have also been discovered. When dinosaurs walked across mud they left tracks behind that became fossils. By looking at these, scientists have discovered how dinosaurs moved and how fast they could run.

Rocks that change

45 When a rock forms in the Earth's crust it may soon be changed again. There are two main ways this can happen. The rock is heated by hot rocks moving up through the crust, or the crust is squashed and heated as mountains form. Both of these ways make crystals in rock change to form new types of rocks, called metamorphic rock.

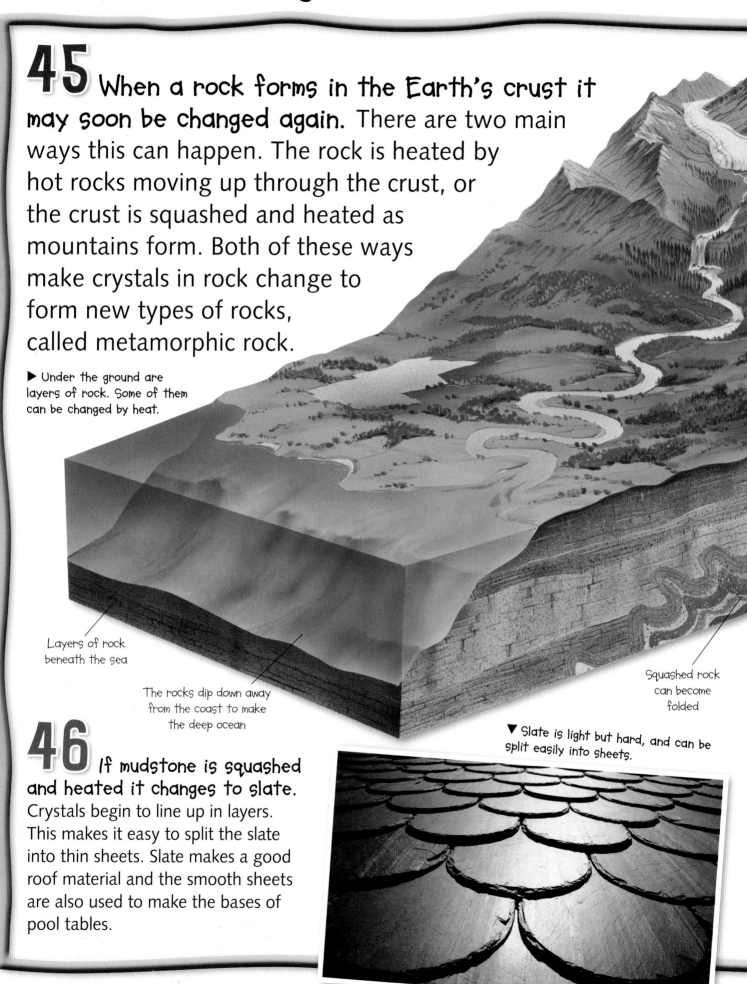

▶ Under the ground are layers of rock. Some of them can be changed by heat.

Layers of rock beneath the sea

The rocks dip down away from the coast to make the deep ocean

Squashed rock can become folded

▼ Slate is light but hard, and can be split easily into sheets.

46 If mudstone is squashed and heated it changes to slate. Crystals begin to line up in layers. This makes it easy to split the slate into thin sheets. Slate makes a good roof material and the smooth sheets are also used to make the bases of pool tables.

Some hot rock travels to the surface through the pipe in a volcano

Layers of rock away from the heat remain unchanged

Hot rock trapped in the crust can change the rock around it

48

Rock can become stripy when it is heated and folded. It becomes so hot, it almost melts. Minerals that make up the rock form layers that appear as coloured stripes. These stripes may be wavy, showing the way the rock has been folded. This type of rock is called gneiss (sounds like 'nice'). Gneiss that is billions of years old has been found under volcanoes in Canada.

▼ The stripes in gneiss are formed by layers of different minerals.

▼ Marble is often used to make ornaments like this Egyptian-style cat.

47

If limestone is heated in the Earth's crust it turns to marble. The shells that make up limestone break up when they are heated strongly and form marble, a rock that has a sugary appearance. The surface of marble can be polished to make it look attractive, and it is used to make statues and ornaments.

QUIZ

1. If a sandstone has red, round, smooth grains, where was the sand made?
2. Which rocks are made from seashells and tiny sea creatures?
3. Name six kinds of dinosaur fossil.
4. Which rock changes into slate?

Answers:
1. The desert 2. Limestone and chalk 3. Bones, teeth, skin, eggs, droppings, tracks 4. Mudstone

Massive mountains

49 **The youngest mountains are the highest.** Young mountains have jagged peaks because softer rocks on the top are broken down by weather. The peaks are made from harder rocks that take longer to break down. In time, even these hard rocks are worn away. This makes an older mountain shorter and gives its top a rounded shape.

▶ It takes millions of years for mountains to form, and the process is happening all the time. A group of mountains is called a range. The biggest ranges are the Alps in Europe, the Andes in South America, the Rockies in North America and the highest of all — the Himalayas in Asia.

50 **When plates in the Earth's crust collide, mountains are formed.** When two continental plates push into each other, the crust at the edge of the plates crumples and folds, pushing up mountain ranges. The Himalayan Mountains in Asia formed in this way.

▼ The Himalayan range contains some of the world's highest mountains, including Mount Everest, the highest of all at 8848 metres.

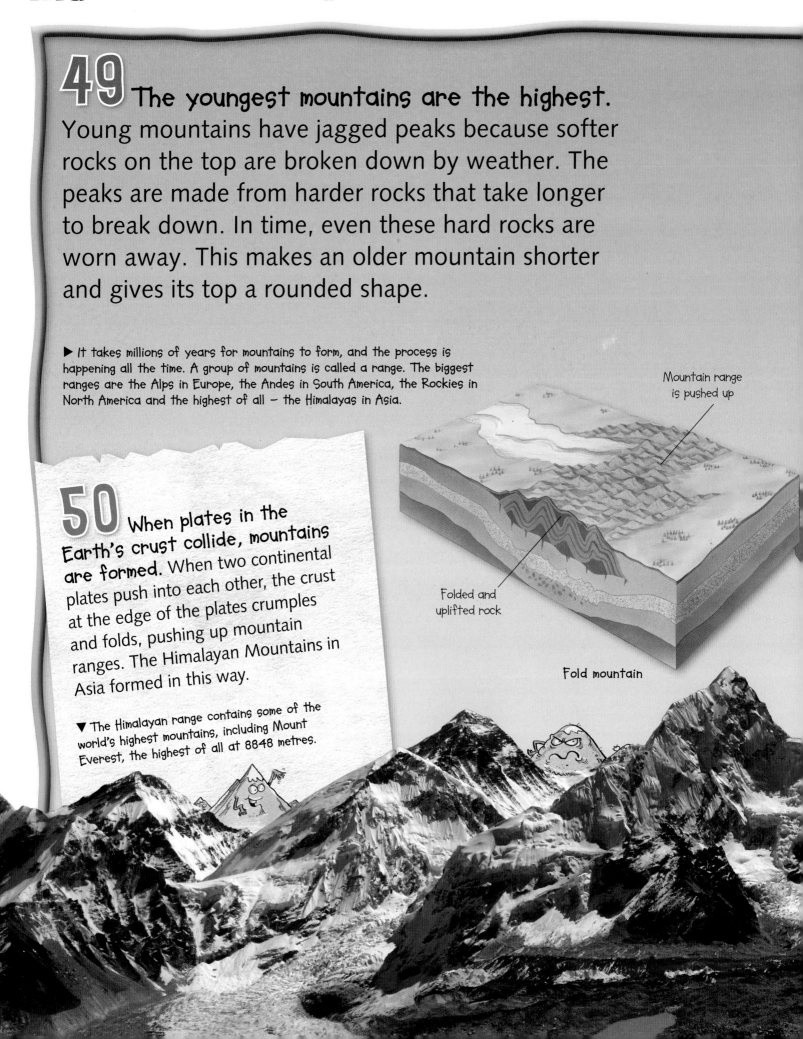

Mountain range is pushed up

Folded and uplifted rock

Fold mountain

51 Some of the Earth's highest mountains are volcanoes. These are formed when molten rock (lava) erupts through the Earth's crust. As the lava cools, it forms a rocky layer. With each new eruption, another layer is added.

Mount Everest 8848 metres

Cerro Aconcagua 6960 metres

Mount Kilimanjaro 5894 metres

Mount McKinley 6194 metres

Mount Cook 3754 metres

Mont Blanc 4809 metres

▲ Mountains are the tallest things on Earth. Mount Cook is the smallest mountain shown here, and it is still four and a half times taller than the world's tallest man-made structure!

Layers of ash and lava build up to form volcanic mountains

Active volcano

Molten rock

Volcanic mountain

Block forced down

Block forced up

Fault

Block mountain

MAKE MOUNTAINS

Put a towel on a table top. Place one hand at either end of the towel. Push your hands together slowly and watch miniature fold mountains form.

52 The movement of the Earth's crust can push blocks of rock upwards to make mountains. When the plates in the crust push together, they produce heat which softens the rock, causing it to fold. Farther away from this heat, cooler rock snaps when it is pushed. The snapped rock makes huge cracks called faults in the crust. When a block of rock between faults is pushed by the rest of the crust, it rises to form a block mountain.

Shaking the Earth

53 An earthquake is caused by violent movements in the Earth's crust. Most occur when two plates in the crust move against each other. An earthquake starts deep underground at its 'focus'. Shock waves move out in all directions, shaking the rock. The point where the shock waves reach the surface is called the epicentre. This is where the strongest shaking takes place.

▼ The focus of an earthquake is the point where the plates suddenly move.

Fault line where two plates move against each other

The epicentre is the point on the surface directly above the focus

Shock waves from the focus

Focus

I DON'T BELIEVE IT!

Since ancient times, people have noticed animals behaving strangely just before earthquakes. Dogs and cats can get agitated, and herds of cattle have been known to run away.

▶ A severely damaged road after the 2010 earthquake in Haiti. Earthquakes can also make buildings collapse, and fire is a hazard, as gas mains can break and catch alight.

54

The power of an earthquake can vary. Half a million earthquakes happen every year but hardly any of these can be felt. About 25 earthquakes each year are powerful enough to cause disasters. Earthquake strength is measured by the Richter Scale. The higher the number on the scale, the more destructive the earthquake.

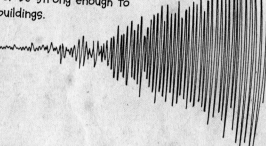

▼ The Richter Scale measures the strength of the shock waves and energy produced by an earthquake. The shock waves can have little effect, or be strong enough to topple buildings.

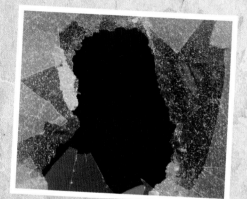

Windows break at level 5

Bridges and buildings collapse at level 7

Widespread destruction occurs at level 8

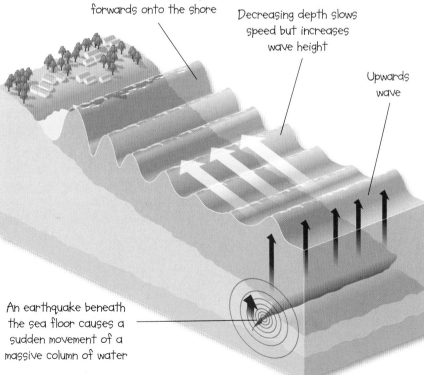

As the tall tsunami reaches shallow water, it surges forwards onto the shore

Decreasing depth slows speed but increases wave height

Upwards wave

An earthquake beneath the sea floor causes a sudden movement of a massive column of water

55

Earthquakes under the sea are called seaquakes. These can cause enormous, devestating waves called tsunamis. As the tsunami rushes across the ocean, it stays quite low. As it reaches the coast, it slows and the water piles up to form a wall. The wave rushes onto the land, destroying everything in its path.

◄ A tsunami can be up to 30 metres high. The weight and power in the wave flattens towns and villages in its path.

Cavernous caves

56 When rain falls on limestone it becomes a cave-maker. Rain water can mix with carbon dioxide to form an acid strong enough to attack limestone and make it dissolve. Underground, the action of the rain water makes caves in which streams, waterfalls and lakes can be found.

▼ Rain water flows through the cracks in limestone and makes them wider to eventually form caves. The horizontal caves are called galleries and the vertical caves are called shafts.

Waterfall in a shaft

Gallery

Cave opening

57 Some caves are made from tubes of lava. As lava moves down the side of a volcano, its surface cools down quickly. The cold lava becomes solid but below, the lava remains warm and keeps flowing. Under the solid surface a tube may form in which liquid lava flows. When the tube empties, a cave is formed.

▶ This cave made by lava in Hawaii is so large that people can walk through it without having to bend down.

58 Dripping water in a limestone cave makes rock spikes. When water drips from a cave roof it leaves a small amount of limestone behind. A spike of rock begins to form. This rock spike, called a stalactite, grows from the ceiling. Where the drops splash onto the cave floor, tiny pieces of limestone gather. They form a spike which points upwards. This is a stalagmite.

59 The longest stalactite is 59 metres long. The tallest stalagmite is 32 metres tall. Over long periods of time, a stalactite and a stalagmite may join together to form a column of rock.

▼ Carlsbad Caverns in New Mexico, USA, are famous for limestone rock formations such as stalactites and stalagmites.

STALACTITES

STALAGMITES

The Earth's treasure

60 Gold can form small grains, large nuggets or veins in rocks. When the rocks wear away, the gold may be found in the sand of river beds. Silver forms branching wires in rock. It does not shine like silver jewellery, but is covered in a black coating called tarnish.

◀ Aluminium must be extracted from its ore — bauxite (shown here) — before it can be used to make all kinds of things, from kitchen foil to aeroplanes.

61 Most metals are found in rocks called ores. An ore is a mixture of different substances, of which metal is one. Each metal has its own ore. For example, aluminium is found in an ore called bauxite. Heat is used to extract metals from their ores. We use metals to make thousands of different things, ranging from watches to jumbo jets.

62 Beautiful crystals can grow in lava bubbles. Lava contains gases which form bubbles. When the lava cools and becomes solid, the bubbles create balloon-shaped spaces in the rock. These are called geodes. Liquids seep into them and form large crystals. The gemstone amethyst forms in this way.

▲ A woman pans for gold in the Mekong River in Southeast Asia.

▲ Inside a geode there is space for crystals to spread out, grow and form perfect shapes.

January
Garnet

February
Amethyst

March
Aquamarine

April
Diamond

May
Emerald

June
Pearl

July
Ruby

August
Peridot

September
Sapphire

October
Opal

63 Gemstones are coloured rocks that are cut and polished to make them sparkle. People have used them to make jewellery for thousands of years. Gems such as topaz, emerald and garnet formed in hot rocks that rose to the Earth's crust and cooled. Most are found as small crystals, but a gem called beryl can have a huge crystal – the largest ever found was 18 metres long! Diamond is a gemstone and is the hardest natural substance found on Earth.

▲ There are more than 100 different kinds of gemstone. Some are associated with different months of the year and are known as 'birthstones'. For example, the birthstone for September is sapphire.

November
Topaz

December
Turquoise

MAKE SALT CRYSTALS

You will need:
table salt
magnifying glass
dark-coloured bowl

Dissolve some table salt in some warm water. Pour the salty water into a dark-coloured bowl. Put the bowl in a warm place so the water can evaporate. After a few days, you can look at the crystals with a magnifying glass.

Lands of sand and grass

64 **The driest places on Earth are deserts.** In many deserts there is a short period of rain each year, but some deserts have completely dry weather for many years. The main deserts of the world are shown on the map.

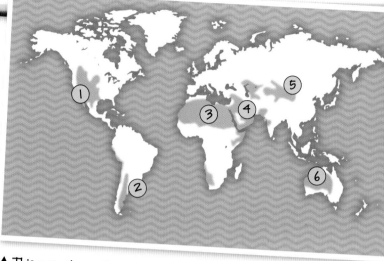

▲ This map shows the major deserts of the world.
① North American deserts – Great Basin and Mojave
② Atacama ③ Sahara ④ Arabian ⑤ Gobi ⑥ Australian deserts – Great Sandy, Gibson, Great Victoria, Simpson

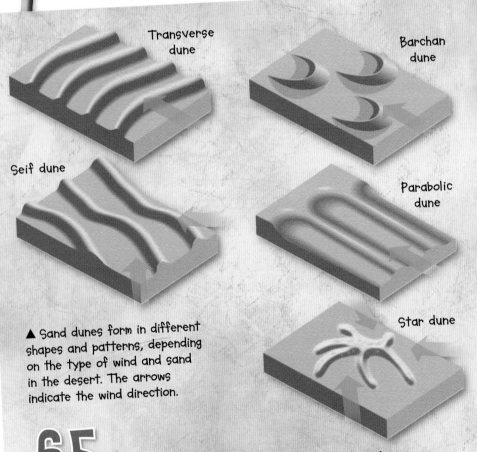

Transverse dune

Barchan dune

Seif dune

Parabolic dune

Star dune

▲ Sand dunes form in different shapes and patterns, depending on the type of wind and sand in the desert. The arrows indicate the wind direction.

65 **Sand dunes are made by winds blowing across a desert.** If there is only a small amount of loose sand on the desert floor, the wind creates crescent-shaped dunes called barchans. If there is plenty of sand, it forms long, straight dunes called transverse dunes. If the wind blows in two directions, it makes long wavy dunes called seif dunes.

66 **Deserts are not always hot.** It can be as hot as 50°C in the day but at night the temperature falls as there is less cloud to trap in heat. Deserts near the Equator have hot days all year round but some deserts farther away have very cold winters.

67 **Camels are adapted for desert life.** Fatty deposits in their humps allow them to live without water for months, and their broad feet stop them sinking into hot sand.

70 Grasslands are found in areas where there is more rain than a desert. They are open spaces where trees rarely grow. Tropical grasslands near the Equator are hot all year round. Grasslands farther away have warm summers and cool winters.

71 Large numbers of animals live on grasslands. In Africa, zebras feed on the top of grass stalks, while gnu eat the middle leaves and gazelles feed on the new shoots. This allows all the animals to feed together. Other animals such as lions feed on the plant-eaters.

▲ Plants and animals can thrive at an oasis in the middle of a desert.

68 An oasis is a pool of water in the desert. It forms from rain water that has seeped into the sand and collected in rocks beneath. The water moves through the rock to where the sand is very thin and forms a pool. Trees and plants grow around the pool and animals visit it to drink.

69 A desert cactus stores water in its stem. The grooves on the stem let it swell with water to keep it alive in the dry weather. The spines stop animals biting into the cactus for a drink.

▶ Different animals can live together by eating grass at differing levels. Zebras ① eat the tall grass. Gnu ② eat the middle shoots and gazelle ③ graze on the lowest shoots.

Fantastic forests

72 There are three main kinds of forest. They are coniferous, temperate and tropical forests. Each grow in different regions of the world, depending on the climate.

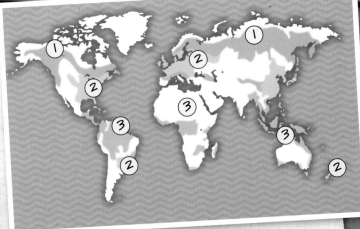

▲ This map shows the major areas of forest in the world:

① Coniferous forest
② Temperate forest
③ Tropical forest

73 Coniferous trees form huge forests around the northern part of the planet. They have long, green, needle-like leaves covered in a waxy coating. These trees stay in leaf throughout the year. In winter, the waxy surface helps snow slide off the leaves so that sunlight can reach them to keep them alive. Coniferous trees produce seeds in cones.

◄ Squirrels can open seed cones from coniferous trees in just a few seconds.

74 Most trees in temperate forests have flat, broad leaves and need large amounts of water to keep them alive. In winter, the trees cannot get enough water from the frozen ground, so they lose their leaves and grow new ones in spring. Deer, rabbits, foxes and mice live on the woodland floor while squirrels, woodpeckers and owls live in the trees.

▲ A jaguar stalks through a dense tropical forest in Belize.

▲ The Hoh temperate rainforest in Washington state, USA, is home to elks, bears and cougars.

75 Large numbers of trees grow close together in a tropical forest. They have broad, evergreen leaves and branches that almost touch. These form a leafy roof over the forest called a canopy. It rains almost every day in a tropical rainforest. The vegetation is so thick, it can take a raindrop ten minutes to reach the ground. Three-quarters of all known animal and plant species live in rainforests. They include huge spiders, brightly coloured frogs and jungle cats.

QUIZ

1. What forms at the top of a cloud?
2. What shape is a barchan sand dune?
3. In which kind of forest would you find brightly coloured frogs?

Answers:
1. Snowflakes 2. Crescent
3. Tropical rainforest

Rivers and lakes

76 **A river can start from a spring.** This is where water flows from the ground. Rain soaks through the ground, and gushes out from the side of a hill. The trickle of water that flows from a spring is called a stream. Many streams join to make a river.

77 **A river changes as it flows to the sea.** Rivers begin in hills and mountains. They are narrow and flow quickly there. When the river flows through flatter land it becomes wider and slow-moving. It makes loops called meanders that may separate and form oxbow lakes. The point where the river meets the sea is the river mouth. This may be a wide channel called an estuary or a group of sandy islands called a delta.

◄ Waterfalls may only be a few centimetres high, or come crashing over a cliff with a massive drop. Angel Falls in Venezuela form the highest falls in the world. One of the drops is an amazing 807 metres.

78 **Water wears rocks down to make a waterfall.** When a river flows from a layer of hard rock onto softer rock, it wears the softer rock down. The rocks and pebbles in the water grind the soft rock away to make a cliff face. At the bottom of the waterfall they make a deep pool called a plunge pool.

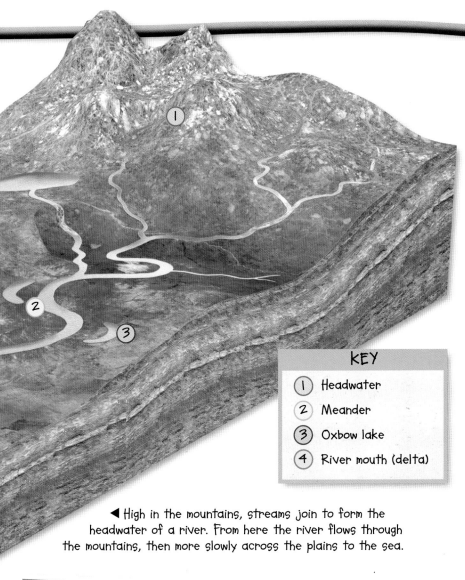

KEY

1. Headwater
2. Meander
3. Oxbow lake
4. River mouth (delta)

◀ High in the mountains, streams join to form the headwater of a river. From here the river flows through the mountains, then more slowly across the plains to the sea.

80 Lakes often form in hollows in the ground. The hollows may be left when glaciers melt or plates in the Earth's crust move apart. Some lakes form when a landslide makes a dam across a river.

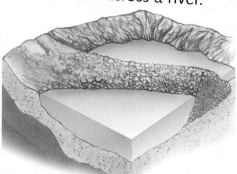

▲ A landslide has fallen into the river and blocked the flow of water to make a lake.

81 A lake can form in the crater of a volcano. A few have also formed in craters left by meteorites that hit Earth long ago.

▼ This lake was formed in a volcanic crater.

◀ Most lakes are blue but some are green, pink, red or even white. The Laguna Colorado in Chile is red due to tiny organisms (creatures) that live in the water.

79 Some lake water can be brightly coloured. The colours are made by tiny organisms called algae or by minerals dissolved in the water.

World of water

82 There is so much water on our planet that it could be called 'Ocean' instead of Earth. Only about one-third of the planet is covered by land. The rest is covered by five huge areas of water called oceans. A sea is a smaller area of water within an ocean. For example, the North Sea is part of the Atlantic Ocean and the Malayan Sea is part of the Pacific Ocean.

83 Coasts are always changing. The point where the sea and land meet is called the coast (1). In many places waves crash onto the land and erode it. Caves (2) and arches (3) are punched into cliffs. In time, the arches break and leave columns of rock called sea stacks (4).

◀ The action of the waves gradually erodes the coastline to create different features.

Continental shelf

Continental slope

84 The oceans are so deep that mountains are hidden beneath them. If you paddle by the shore the water is quite shallow, but at its deepest point, the ocean reaches 10,911 metres. The ocean floor is a flat plain with mountain ranges rising across it. These mark where two tectonic plates meet. Nearer the coast are deep trenches where the edges of two plates have moved apart. Extinct volcanoes form mountains called seamounts.

▼ Corals only grow in tropical or sub-tropical waters. They tend to grow in shallow water where there is lots of sunlight.

85
Tiny creatures can make islands in the oceans. Coral is made from the leftover skeletons of sea creatures called polyps. Over millions of years the skeletons build up to form huge coral reefs. Coral also builds up to create islands around extinct volcanoes in the Pacific and Indian Oceans.

86
There are thousands of icebergs floating in the oceans. They are made from glaciers and ice sheets which have formed at the North and South Poles. Only about a tenth of an iceberg can be seen above water. The rest lies below and can damage and sink ships that sail too close.

▶ Under every iceberg is a huge amount of ice, usually much bigger than the area visible from the surface.

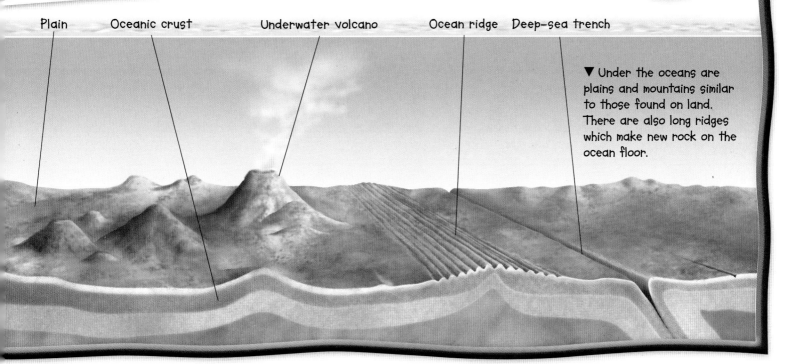

Plain   Oceanic crust   Underwater volcano   Ocean ridge   Deep-sea trench

▼ Under the oceans are plains and mountains similar to those found on land. There are also long ridges which make new rock on the ocean floor.

The planet of life

87 There are millions of different kinds of life forms on Earth. So far, life has not been found anywhere else. Living things survive here because it is warm, there is water and the air contains oxygen. If we discover other planets with these conditions, there may be life on them too.

▼ Despite being the biggest fish in the oceans, the mighty whale shark feeds on tiny shrimp-like creatures.

88 The star-nosed mole has feelers on the end of its nose. It uses them to find food.

89 Many living things on the Earth are tiny. They are so small that we cannot see them. A whale shark is the largest fish on the planet, yet it feeds on tiny shrimp-like creatures. These in turn feed on even smaller plant-like organisms called plankton, which make food from sunlight and sea water. Microscopic bacteria are found in the soil and even on your skin.

▼ This caterpillar eats as much plant life as possible before beginning its change to a butterfly.

90 Animals cannot live without plants. A plant makes food from sunlight, water, air and minerals in the soil. Animals cannot make their own food so many of them eat plants. Others survive by eating the plant-eaters. If plants died out, all the animals would die too.

91
The air can be full of animals.
On a warm day, clouds of midges and
gnats form close to the ground. In spring
and autumn, flocks of birds fly to different
parts of the world to nest. On summer
evenings bats hunt for midges flying in
the air.

92
**The surface of the ground
is home to many small animals.** Mice
scurry through the grass. Larger
animals such as deer hide in bushes.
The elephant is the largest land animal.
It does not need to hide because
few animals would attack it.

93
**If you dig into the ground
you can find animals living there.** The
earthworm is a common creature found in
the soil. It feeds on rotting plants that it
pulls into the soil. Earthworms are eaten
by moles that dig their way underground.

▲ Animals thrive in many different
kinds of habitats on Earth. The skies,
the ground and even underground are
home to countless forms of life.

Caring for the planet

94 **Many useful materials come from the Earth.** These make clothes, buildings, furniture and containers such as cans. Some materials, like those used to make buildings, last a long time. Others, such as those used to make cans, may be used up on the day they are bought.

Factories pump out chemicals that can cause acid rain. They also dump polluted water in rivers amd seas.

95 **We may run out of some materials in the future.** Metals are found in rocks called ores. When all the ore has been used up we will not be able to make new metal. We must be careful not to use too much wood, as although new trees are always being planted, they may not grow fast enough for our needs, and we could run out.

96 **We can make materials last longer by recycling them.** Metal, glass and plastic are often thrown away and buried in a tip after they have been used. Today more people recycle materials. This means sending them back to factories to be used again.

◄ Sorting waste into different materials before it is collected makes recycling more efficient.

▼ Here are some of the ways in which we are harming our planet today. We must think of better ways to treat the Earth in the future.

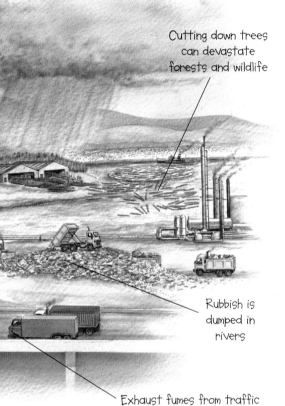

Cutting down trees can devastate forests and wildlife

Rubbish is dumped in rivers

Exhaust fumes from traffic clog up the atmosphere

97 Air and water can be polluted by our activities. Burning coal and oil for electricity makes fumes which can make rain water acidic. This can kill trees and damage soil. Chemicals from factories are sometimes released into rivers and seas, endangering wildlife.

98 Living things can be protected. Large areas of land have been made into national parks where wildlife is protected. People can come to study, observe and enjoy plants and animals.

99 We use huge amounts of fuel. The main fuels are coal and oil, which are used to make electricity. Oil is also used in petrol for cars. In time, these fuels will run out. Scientists are developing ways of using other energy sources such as wind power. Huge wind turbines are already used to make electricity.

100 The Earth is nearly five billion years old. From a ball of molten rock it has grown into a living, breathing planet. We must try to keep it that way. Switching off lights to save energy and picking up litter are things we can all do to protect our planet.

▶ In a wind turbine, the spinning movement is changed into electrical energy.

I DON'T BELIEVE IT!

By the middle of the 21st century 30 to 50 percent of all living species may be extinct.

OCEANS

ATLANTIC OCEAN

PACIFIC OCEAN

101 Oceans cover more than two-thirds of the Earth's rocky surface. Their total area is about 362 million square kilometres, which means there is more than twice as much ocean as land! Although all the oceans flow into each other, we know them as five different oceans – the Pacific, Atlantic, Indian, Southern and Arctic. Our landmasses, the continents, rise out of the oceans.

102 The largest, deepest ocean is the Pacific. It covers nearly half of our planet and is double the size of the Atlantic, the next largest ocean. In places, the Pacific is so deep that the Earth's tallest mountain, Everest, would sink without a trace.

▼ The point where the ocean meets the land is called the seashore.

103 Oceans can look blue, green or grey. This is because of the way light hits the surface. Water soaks up the red parts of light but scatters the blue-green parts, making the sea look different shades of blue or green.

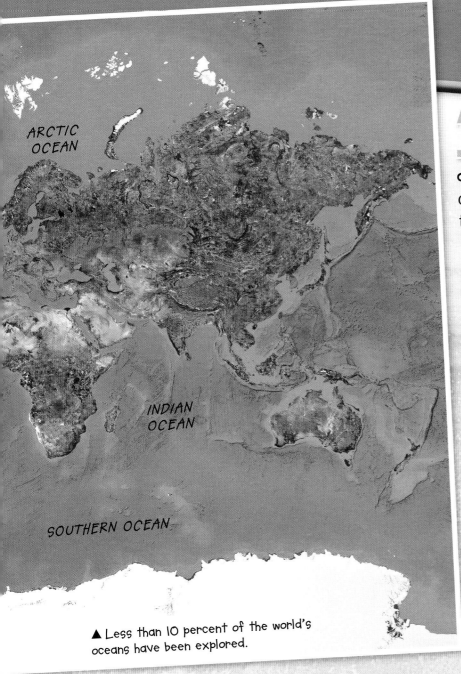

ARCTIC OCEAN

INDIAN OCEAN

SOUTHERN OCEAN

▲ Less than 10 percent of the world's oceans have been explored.

104 **Seas can be red or dead.** A sea is a small part of an ocean. The Red Sea, for example, is the part of the Indian Ocean between Egypt and Saudi Arabia. Asia's Dead Sea gets its name because it is so salty that living things can't survive there.

105 **There are streams in the oceans.** All the water in the oceans is constantly moving, but in some places it flows as currents, which take particular paths. One of these is the warm Gulf Stream, that travels around the edge of the Atlantic Ocean.

I DON'T BELIEVE IT!
Oceans hold 97 percent of the world's water. Just a fraction is in freshwater lakes and rivers.

Ocean features

106 There are plains, mountains and valleys under the oceans, in areas called basins. Each basin has a rim (the flat continental shelf that meets the shore) and sides (the continental slope that drops away from the shelf). In the ocean basin there are flat abyssal plains, steep hills, huge underwater volcanoes called seamounts, and deep valleys called trenches.

Continental slope

Land

Continental shelf

Spreading ridge

▼ As the magma (molten rock) cools, the ocean floor spreads out.

Spreading floor

Ridge

Magma

Abyssal trench

Abyssal hills

▲ Under the oceans there is a landscape similar to that found on land.

107 The ocean floor is spreading. Molten (liquid) rock inside the Earth seeps from holes on the seabed. As the rock cools, it forms new sections of floor that creep slowly out. Scientists have proved this fact by looking at layers of rock on the ocean floor. There are matching stripes of rock either side of a ridge. Each pair came from the same hot rock eruption, then slowly spread out.

Seamount

Volcanic island

Ocean trench

109

Some islands are swallowed by the ocean. Sometimes, a ring-shaped coral reef called an atoll marks where a volcanic island once was. The coral reef built up around the island. After the volcano sank underwater, the reef remained.

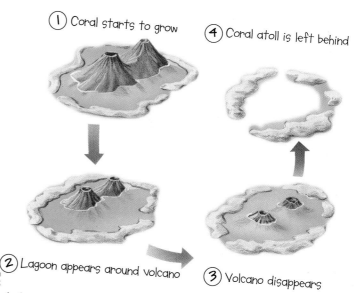

① Coral starts to grow

④ Coral atoll is left behind

② Lagoon appears around volcano

③ Volcano disappears

▲ An atoll is a ring-shaped coral reef that encloses a deep lagoon. It is left when an island sinks underwater.

110

New islands are born all the time. When an underwater volcano erupts, its lava cools in the water. Layers of lava build up, and the volcano grows in size. Eventually, it is tall enough to peep above the waves. The Hawaiian islands rose from the sea like this.

108

The world's longest mountain chain is under the ocean. It is the Mid-Ocean range and stretches around the middle of the Earth.

▶ The Hawaiian islands were built up from layers of lava. There are still more to come.

Tides and shores

111 The sea level rises and falls twice each day along the coast. This is known as high and low tides. Tides happen because of the pull of the Moon's gravity, which lifts water from the part of Earth's surface facing it.

▼ At high tide, the sea rises up the shore and dumps seaweed, shells and driftwood. Most coasts have two high tides and two low tides every day.

High tides happen at the same time each day on opposite sides of the Earth

At high tide the water level rises

At low tide the water level goes down again

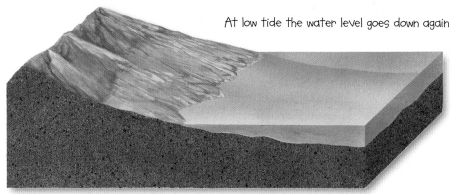

112 Spring tides are especially high. They occur twice a month, when the Moon is in line with the Earth and the Sun. Then, the Sun's pulling force joins the Moon's and seawater is lifted higher than usual. The opposite happens when the Moon and Sun are at right angles to each other. Then, their pulling powers work against each other causing weak neap tides – the lowest high tides and low tides.

▶ Spring tides occur when the Sun and the Moon are lined up and pulling together.

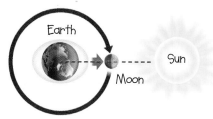

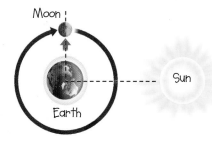

◀ Neap tides occur when the Sun and Moon are at right angles to each other and pulling in different directions.

113
The sea is strong enough to carve into rock. Pounding waves batter coastlines and erode, or wear away, the rock.

▼ Erosion can create amazing shapes such as arches, and pillars called sea stacks.

Sea stack

Arch

114
Sand is found on bars and spits, as well as beaches. It is made up of grains of worn-down rock and shell. Sand collects on shorelines and spits, but also forms on offshore beaches called sand bars. Spits are narrow ridges of worn sand and pebbles.

115
Some shores are swampy. This makes the border between land and sea hard to pinpoint. Muddy coastlines include tropical mangrove swamps that are flooded by salty water from the sea.

▶ The stilt roots of mangrove trees can take in nutrients from the water.

I DON'T BELIEVE IT!

The biggest tsunami was taller than five Statues of Liberty! It hit the Japanese Ryuku Islands in 1771.

116
Tsunamis are the most powerful waves. They happen when underwater earthquakes trigger tremendous shock waves. These whip up a wall of water that travels across the ocean's surface.

Life in a rock pool

117 Rock pools are teeming with all kinds of creatures. Limpets are a kind of shellfish. They live on rocks and in pools at shorelines. Here, they eat slimy, green algae, but they have to withstand the crashing tide. They cling to the rock with their muscular foot, only moving when the tide is out.

QUIZ

Can you find the names of four shells in the puzzle below?
1. alcm 2. lesmus
3. teroys 4. hewkl

Answers:
1. Clam 2. Mussel
3. Oyster 4. Whelk

118 Some anemones fight with harpoons. Beadlet anemones will sometimes fight over a feeding ground. Their weapon is the poison they usually use to stun their prey. They shoot tiny hooks like harpoons at each other until the weakest one gives in.

▶ Anemones are named after flowers, because of their petal–like arms.

▶ Starfish are relatives of brittle stars, sea urchins and sea cucumbers.

119 Starfish can grow new arms. They may have as many as 40 arms, or rays. If a predator grabs hold of one, the starfish abandons the ray, and uses the others to make its getaway!

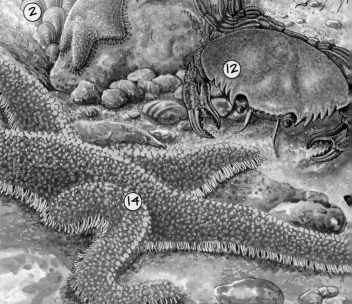

120 Hermit crabs do not have shells.

Most crabs shed their shells as they outgrow them, but the hermit crab does not have a shell. It borrows the leftover shell of a dead whelk or other mollusc – whatever it can squeeze into to protect its soft body. These crabs have even been spotted using a coconut shell as a home!

▶ Hermit crabs protect their soft bodies in a borrowed shell.

121 Sea urchins wear a disguise.

Green sea urchins sometimes drape themselves with bits of shell, pebble and seaweed. This makes the urchin more difficult for predators, or hunters, to spot.

122 Sponges are animals!

They are very simple creatures that filter food from seawater. The natural sponge that you might use in the bath is a long-dead, dried-out sponge.

◀ There are about 4500 different types of sponge in the sea.

Colourful coral

123 Tiny animals build huge underwater walls. These are built up from coral, the leftover skeletons of sea creatures called polyps. Over millions of years, enough skeletons pile up to form huge, wall-like structures called reefs. Coral reefs are full of hidey-holes and make brilliant habitats for all sorts of amazing, colourful sea life.

▲ The Great Barrier Reef in Australia is the world's largest coral reef.

125 The world's biggest shellfish lives on coral reefs. Giant clams grow to well over one metre long – big enough for you to bathe in its shell!

124 Male seahorses have the babies. They don't exactly give birth, but they store the eggs in a pouch on their belly. When the eggs are ready to hatch, a stream of miniature seahorses billows out from the male's pouch.

◄ Baby seahorses stream out of the male's pouch and into the sea.

Parrot fish

Giant clam

126 Some fish go to the cleaners.

Cleaner wrasse are little fish that are paid for cleaning! Larger fish, such as groupers and moray eels visit the wrasse, which eat all the parasites and other bits of dirt off the bigger fishes' bodies – what a feast!

127 Clownfish are sting-proof.

Most creatures steer clear of an anemone's stinging tentacles. But the clownfish swims among the stingers, where it's safe from predators. Strangely, the anemone doesn't seem to sting the clownfish.

128 Some fish look like stones.

Stone fish rest on the seabed, looking just like the rocks that surround them. If they are spotted, the poisonous spines on their backs can stun an attacker in seconds.

129 You can see the Great Barrier Reef from space!

At over 2000 kilometres long, it is the largest structure ever built by living creatures.

Lion fish

Cleaner wrasse fish

Clownfish

Stone fish

▲ Tropical coral reefs are the habitat of an amazing range of marine plants and creatures.

Swimming machines

130 There are over 21,000 different types of fish in the sea. They range from huge whale sharks to tiny gobies. Almost all are covered in scales and use fins and a muscular tail to power through the water. Like their freshwater cousins, sea fish have slits called gills that take oxygen from the water so they can breathe.

▶ In a large group called a school, fish like these yellow snappers have less chance of being picked off by a predator.

131 The oarfish is bigger than an oar – it can be as long as four canoes! It is the longest bony fish and is found in all the world's oceans. Oarfish are striking creatures – they have a red fin along the length of their back.

◀ People once thought oarfish swam horizontally through the water. Now they know they swim upright.

132 Sunfish like sunbathing! Ocean sunfish are very large, broad fish that can weigh up to one tonne. They are named after their habit of sunbathing on the surface of the ocean.

◀ At over 3 metres long, sunfish are the biggest bony fish in the oceans. They feed on plankton.

133 **Flying fish cannot really fly.** Fish can't survive out of water, but flying fish sometimes leap above the waves when they are travelling at high speeds. They use their wing-like fins to keep them in the air for as long as 30 seconds.

▲ Flying fish feed near the surface so they are easy to find. Their gliding flight helps them escape most hunters.

QUIZ

1. Which fish like to sunbathe?
2. How many types of fish live in the sea?
3. How does a fish breathe?
4. Can flying fish really fly?

Answers:
1. Sunfish 2. Over 21,000 3. With its gills 4. No

134 **Not all fish are the same shape.** Cod or mackerel are what we think of as a normal fish shape, but fish come in all shapes and sizes. Flounder and other flatfish have squashed-flat bodies. Eels are so long and thin that the biggest types look like snakes, while tiny garden eels resemble worms! And of course, seahorses and seadragons look nothing like other fish at all!

▶ The flounder's flattened shape and dull colouring help to camouflage (hide) it on the seabed.

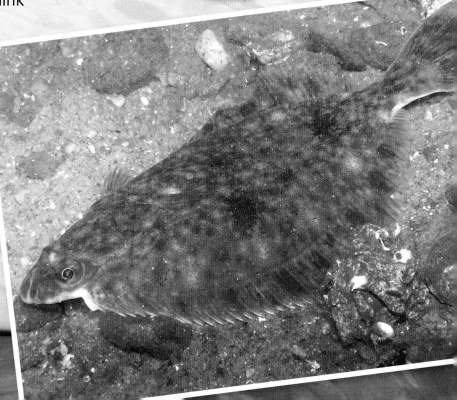

Shark!

▼ Great white sharks are fierce hunters. They will attack and eat almost anything, but prefer to feed on seals.

135 Great whites are the scariest sharks in the oceans. These powerful predators have been known to kill people and can speed through the water at 30 kilometres an hour. Unlike most fish, the great white is warm-blooded. This allows its muscles to work well, but also means the shark has to feed on plenty of meat.

▶ Basking sharks eat enormous amounts of plankton, which they sieve from the water as they swim.

136 Most sharks are meat-eaters. Herring are a favourite food for sand tiger and thresher sharks, while a tiger shark will eat just about anything! Strangely, some of the biggest sharks take the smallest prey. Whale sharks and basking sharks eat tiny sea creatures called plankton.

137 Sharks are shaped like torpedos.

Most sharks are built for speed, with a long streamlined body. This means water can move past them easily. A shark's fins keep it the right way up in the water, and help it to change direction quickly, so it can chase its prey. Sharks also have special cells in their heads, called ampullae of Lorenzini. These allow them to sense electricity given out by nearby fish.

I DON'T BELIEVE IT!
Some sharks, such as dogfish and zebra sharks, don't look after their pups. They leave them to fend for themselves.

Nostril

Dorsal fin

Jaw

Ampullae of Lorenzini

Gill

▶ The different features of a shark's body help it to be a successful hunter.

Pectoral fin

Pelvic fin

Anal fin

Tail fin

138 Hammerhead sharks have a hammer-shaped head! With a nostril and an eye on each end of the 'hammer', they swing their head from side to side. This gives them double the chance to see and sniff out any signs of a tasty catch.

▲ Hammerheads prey on other sharks and rays, bony fish, crabs and lobsters, octopus and squid.

Whales and dolphins

139 The biggest animal on the planet lives in the oceans. It is the blue whale, measuring about 28 metres in length and weighing up to 190 tonnes. It feeds by filtering tiny, shrimp-like creatures called krill from the water – about four tonnes of krill a day! Like other great whales, it has special, sieve-like parts in its mouth called baleen plates.

► The blue whale can be found in every ocean except the Arctic.

140 Killer whales play with their food. They especially like to catch baby seals, which they toss into the air before eating. Killer whales are not true whales, but the largest dolphins. They have teeth for chewing, instead of baleen plates.

▼ As the sperm whale surfaces, it pushes out stale air through its blowhole. It fills its lungs with fresh air and dives down again.

141 Whales and dolphins have to come to the surface for air. This is because they are mammals, like we are. Sperm whales hold their breath the longest. They have been known to stay underwater for nearly two hours.

142

Dolphins and whales sing songs to communicate. The noisiest is the humpback whale, whose wailing noises can be heard for hundreds of kilometres. The sweetest is the beluga – nicknamed the 'sea canary'. Songs are used to attract a mate, or just to keep track of each other.

▲ The beluga is a type of white whale. It makes a range of noises – whistles, clangs, chirps and moos!

144

Moby-Dick was a famous white whale. It featured in *Moby-Dick* (1851), a book by Herman Melville about a white sperm whale and a whaler called Captain Ahab.

143

The narwhal has a horn like a unicorn's. This Arctic whale has a long, twirly tooth that spirals out of its head. The males use their tusks as a weapon when they are fighting over females.

I DON'T BELIEVE IT!

Barnacles are shellfish. They attach themselves to ships' hulls, or the bodies of grey whales and other large sea animals.

▲ A male narwhal's tusk can grow to over 2 metres long.

Sleek swimmers

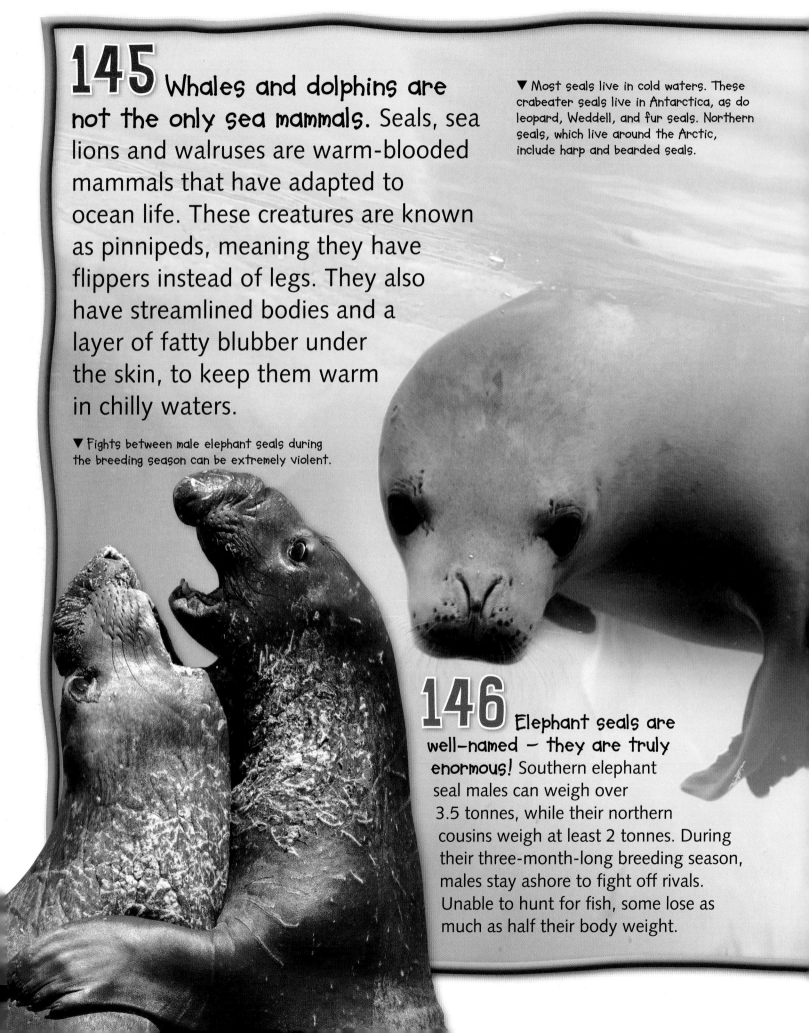

145 **Whales and dolphins are not the only sea mammals.** Seals, sea lions and walruses are warm-blooded mammals that have adapted to ocean life. These creatures are known as pinnipeds, meaning they have flippers instead of legs. They also have streamlined bodies and a layer of fatty blubber under the skin, to keep them warm in chilly waters.

▼ Fights between male elephant seals during the breeding season can be extremely violent.

▼ Most seals live in cold waters. These crabeater seals live in Antarctica, as do leopard, Weddell, and fur seals. Northern seals, which live around the Arctic, include harp and bearded seals.

146 **Elephant seals are well-named – they are truly enormous!** Southern elephant seal males can weigh over 3.5 tonnes, while their northern cousins weigh at least 2 tonnes. During their three-month-long breeding season, males stay ashore to fight off rivals. Unable to hunt for fish, some lose as much as half their body weight.

147

Walruses seem to change colour! When a walrus is in the water, it appears pale brown or even white. This is because blood drains from the skin's surface to stop the body losing heat. On land, the blood returns to the skin and walruses can look reddish brown or pink.

▼ Walruses use their tusks as weapons. They are also used to make breathing holes in the ice, and to help the walrus pull itself out of the water.

148

Leopard seals sing in their sleep! These seals, found in the Antarctic, chirp and whistle while they snooze.

149

Sea otters anchor themselves when they sleep. These playful creatures live off the Pacific coast among huge forests of giant seaweed called kelp. When they sleep, they wrap a strand of kelp around their body to stop them being washed out to sea.

▼ Anchored to the kelp, a sea otter is free to rest.

Ocean reptiles

150 Marine iguanas are the most seaworthy lizards. Most lizards prefer life on land, where it is easier to warm up their cold-blooded bodies, but marine iguanas depend on the sea for food. They dive underwater to graze. When on land, the iguanas' dark skin absorbs the Sun's heat.

▼ Marine iguanas are found around the Galapagos Islands in the Pacific. They dive into the water to graze on seaweed and the algae growing on rocks.

▼ Female green turtles use their flippers to dig a large nest. Once they have laid their eggs, they cover the nest with sand.

151 Turtles come ashore only to lay their eggs. Although they are born on land, turtles head for the sea the minute they hatch. Females return to the beach where they were born to dig their nests. After they have laid their eggs, they go straight back to the water. Hawksbill turtles may lay up to 140 eggs in a clutch, while some green turtle females clock up 800 eggs in a year!

QUIZ

1. Where are marine iguanas found?
2. Why do turtles come ashore?
3. Where do banded sea snakes search for food?
4. How deep can leatherback turtles dive?

Answers:
1. Around the Galapagos Islands
2. To lay their eggs 3. Coral reefs
4. Up to 1200 metres

152
There are venomous (poisonous) snakes in the sea. Most stay close to land and come ashore to lay their eggs. Banded sea snakes, for example, cruise around coral reefs in search of their favourite food – eels. But the yellow-bellied sea snake never leaves the water. It gives birth to live babies in the open ocean.

▶ Banded sea snakes use venom (poison) to stun their prey.

▼ The yellow-bellied sea snake uses its colourful underside to attract fish. It then darts back – so the fish are next to its open mouth!

Banded sea snake

Yellow-bellied sea snake

153
Leatherback turtles dive up to 1200 metres for food. They hold the record for being the biggest sea turtles and for making the deepest dives. Leatherbacks feed mostly on jellyfish but their diet also includes molluscs, crabs, lobsters and starfish.

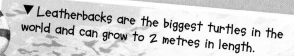
▼ Leatherbacks are the biggest turtles in the world and can grow to 2 metres in length.

Icy depths

154 Few creatures can survive in the dark, icy-cold ocean depths. Food is so hard to come by, the deep-sea anglerfish does not waste energy chasing prey. It has a stringy 'fishing rod' with a glowing tip that extends from its dorsal fin or hangs above its jaw. This attracts smaller fish to the anglerfish's big mouth.

▲ Anglerfish are black or brown for camouflage. Only their glowing 'fishing rod' is visible in the gloom.

Lantern fish

Cookie-cutter shark

Hatchet fish

155 Some deep-sea fish glow in the dark. As well as tempting prey, light also confuses predators. About 1500 different deep-sea fish give off light. The lantern fish's whole body glows. The hatchet fish produces light along its belly and has silvery scales on its sides, which reflect light, confusing predators. Just the belly of the cookie-cutter shark gives off a ghostly glow.

◄ The light created by deep-sea fish, or by bacteria living on their bodies, is known as biological light, or bioluminescence.

156 Black
swallowers are greedy-
guts! These strange fish are
just 25 centimetres long but
can eat fish far bigger than
themselves. Their loose jaws
unhinge to fit over the prey.
Then the stretchy body
expands to take in their
enormous meal.

157 Viperfish have
teeth that are invisible in
the dark. They swim around
with their jaws wide open.
Deep-sea shrimp often see
nothing until they are right
inside the viperfish's mouth.

▶ The viperfish is named for its long,
snake-like fangs.

▲ The black swallower's stomach can
stretch to take in prey twice its length.

158 On the seabed, there are worms
as long as cars! These are giant tubeworms
and they cluster around hot spots on the ocean
floor. They feed on tiny particles that they filter
from the water.

▼ Bacteria inside the tubeworm
turn minerals into food that the
worm needs to survive.

Plume

Bacteria

Heart

Blood
Vessel

Tube

I DON'T BELIEVE IT!
Female deep-sea anglerfish
grow to 120 centimetres in
length, but the males are a
tiny 6 centimetres!

67

Amazing journeys

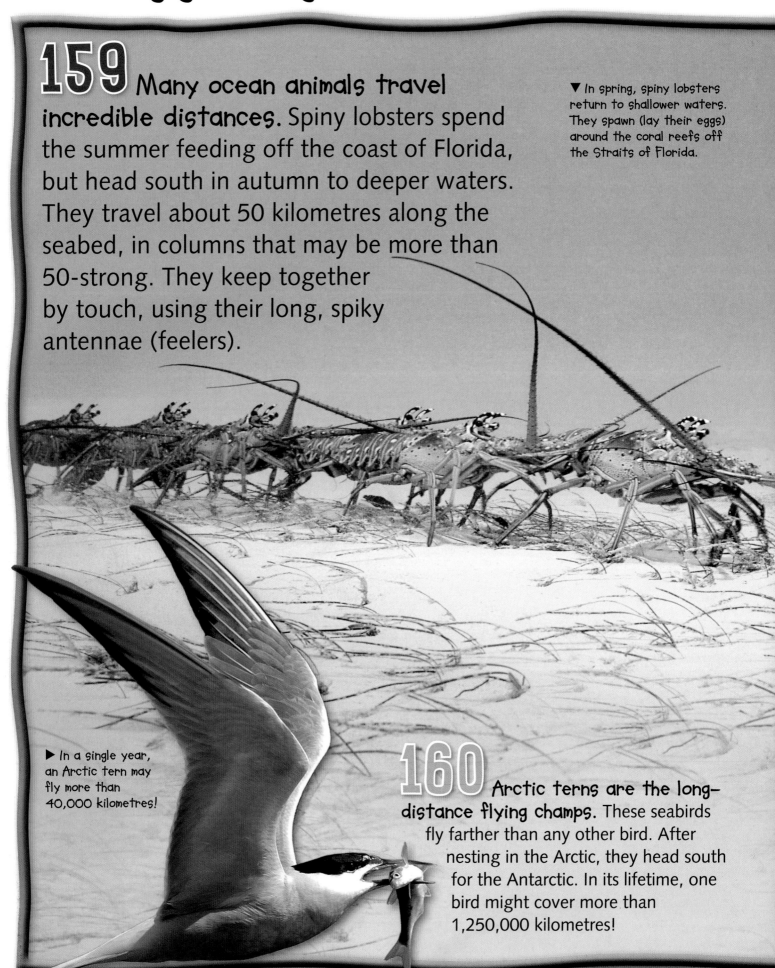

159 **Many ocean animals travel incredible distances.** Spiny lobsters spend the summer feeding off the coast of Florida, but head south in autumn to deeper waters. They travel about 50 kilometres along the seabed, in columns that may be more than 50-strong. They keep together by touch, using their long, spiky antennae (feelers).

▼ In spring, spiny lobsters return to shallower waters. They spawn (lay their eggs) around the coral reefs off the Straits of Florida.

▶ In a single year, an Arctic tern may fly more than 40,000 kilometres!

160 **Arctic terns are the long-distance flying champs.** These seabirds fly farther than any other bird. After nesting in the Arctic, they head south for the Antarctic. In its lifetime, one bird might cover more than 1,250,000 kilometres!

● Grey whales travel south to Mexico in winter to have their babies

② In summer the whales swim back to the food-rich waters off the coast of Alaska

▲ Grey whales spend summer in the Bering Sea, feeding on tiny, shrimp-like creatures called amphipods. They spend their breeding season, December to March, in warmer waters.

162 Grey whales migrate, or travel, farther than any other mammal. There are two main grey whale populations in the Pacific. One spends summer off the Alaskan coast. In winter they migrate south to Mexico to breed. The whales may swim nearly 20,000 kilometres in a year. The other grey whale group spends summer off the coast of Russia, then travels south to Korea.

163 When it's time to spawn (lay their eggs) eels and salmon return to the river nurseries where they were born. This migration from the open ocean covers hundreds or even thousands of kilometres.

▲ As soon as they are born, loggerhead hatchlings crawl down to the water, to avoid being picked off by hungry gulls or crabs.

161 Baby loggerhead turtles make a two-year journey. They are born on beaches in Japan. The hatchlings hurry down to the sea and set off across the Pacific to Mexico, a journey of 10,000 kilometres. They spend about five years there before returning to Japan to breed.

On the wing

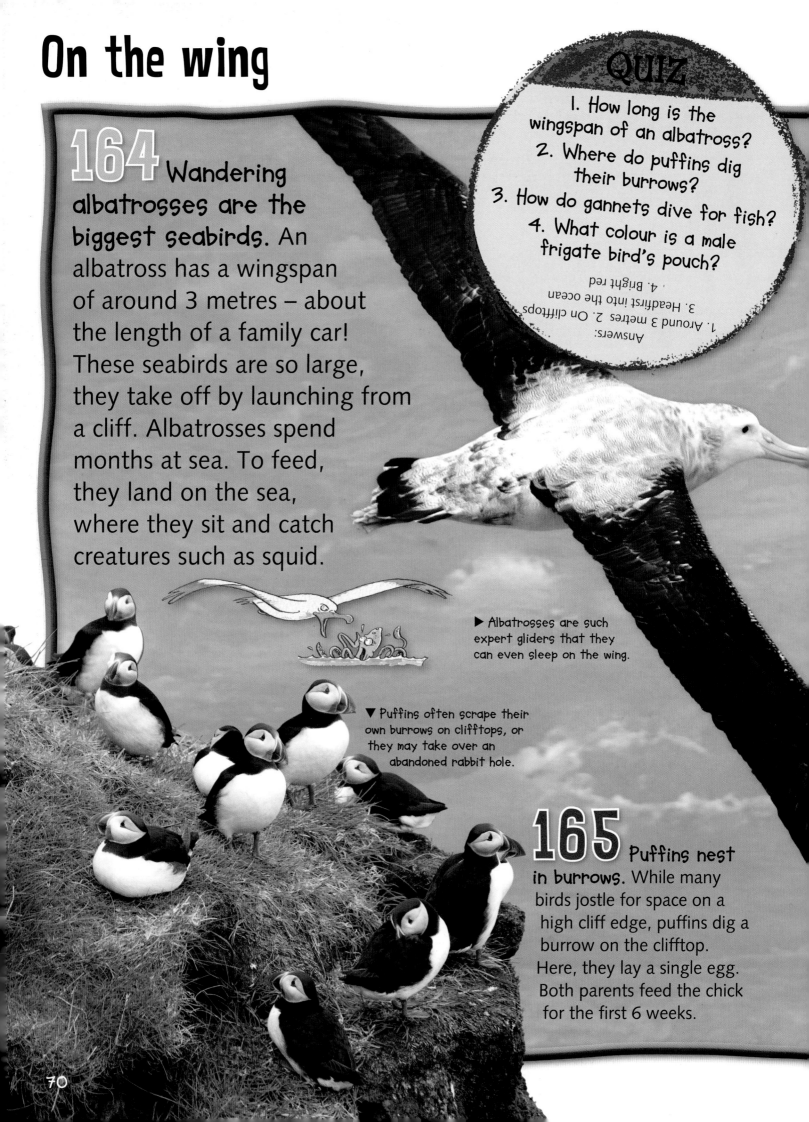

164 Wandering albatrosses are the biggest seabirds. An albatross has a wingspan of around 3 metres – about the length of a family car! These seabirds are so large, they take off by launching from a cliff. Albatrosses spend months at sea. To feed, they land on the sea, where they sit and catch creatures such as squid.

QUIZ

1. How long is the wingspan of an albatross?
2. Where do puffins dig their burrows?
3. How do gannets dive for fish?
4. What colour is a male frigate bird's pouch?

Answers:
1. Around 3 metres 2. On clifftops
3. Headfirst into the ocean
4. Bright red

▶ Albatrosses are such expert gliders that they can even sleep on the wing.

▼ Puffins often scrape their own burrows on clifftops, or they may take over an abandoned rabbit hole.

165 Puffins nest in burrows. While many birds jostle for space on a high cliff edge, puffins dig a burrow on the clifftop. Here, they lay a single egg. Both parents feed the chick for the first 6 weeks.

166 Gannets wear air-bag shock absorbers. The gannet's feeding technique is to plummet headfirst into the ocean and catch a fish in its beak. It dives at high-speed and hits the water hard. Luckily, the gannet's head is protected with sacs of air that absorb most of the shock.

167 Frigate birds puff up a balloon for their mate. Male frigate birds have a bright-red pouch on their throat. They inflate, or blow up, the pouch as part of their display to attract a female.

▲ When a gannet spots its meal, it dives into the water at high speed to catch it.

▼ A frigate bird shows off to its mate.

▶ A blue-footed booby displays its blue feet.

168 Boobies dance to attract a mate. There are two types of booby, blue- or red-footed. The dancing draws attention to the male's colourful feet. Perhaps this stops the females from mating with the wrong type of bird.

Perfect penguins

169 Macaroni, Chinstrap, Jackass and Emperor are all types of penguin. There are 17 different types in total, and most live around the Antarctic. Penguins feed on fish, squid and krill. Their black-and-white plumage is important camouflage. Seen from above, a penguin's black back blends in with the water. The white belly is hard to distinguish from the sunlit surface of the sea.

170 Penguins can swim, but not fly. They have oily, waterproofed feathers and flipper-like wings. Instead of lightweight, hollow bones – like a flying bird's – some penguins have solid, heavy bones. This enables them to stay underwater longer when diving for food. Emperor penguins can stay under for 15 minutes or more.

171 Some penguins build stone circles. This is the way that Adélie and Gentoo penguins build nests on the shingled shores where they breed. First, they scrape out a small dip with their flippered feet and then they surround the hollow with a circle of pebbles.

▲ An Adélie penguin builds its nest from stones and small rocks.

▼ King penguins live near Antarctica. Like all penguins, they have a layer of fat under their feathers to protect them in the icy water.

▼ The different types of penguin vary in shape, size and appearance.

Rockhopper   Macaroni   Royal   Chinstrap   Gentoo

I DON'T BELIEVE IT!

The fastest swimming bird is the Gentoo penguin. It has been known to swim at speeds of 27 kilometres an hour!

172 **Emperor penguin dads balance an egg on their feet.** They do this to keep their egg off the Antarctic ice, where it would freeze. The female leaves her mate with the egg for the whole two months that it takes to hatch. The male has to go without food during this time. When the chick hatches, the mother returns and both parents help to raise it.

▶ A downy Emperor penguin chick cannot find its own food in the sea until it has grown its waterproof, adult plumage. In the meantime, its parents feed and care for it.

Harvests from the sea

173 Oysters come from beds – and lobsters from pots! The animals in the oceans feed other sea creatures, and they feed us, too! To gather oysters, fishermen raise them on trays or poles in the water. First, they collect oyster larvae, or babies. They attract them by putting out sticks hung with shells. Lobster larvae are too difficult to collect, but the adults are caught in pots filled with fish bait.

▲ Bait is placed in lobster pots like these. Once a lobster has entered, it can't escape.

174 Some farmers grow seaweed. Seaweed is delicious to eat, and is also a useful ingredient in products such as ice cream and plant fertilizer. In shallow, tropical waters, people grow their own on plots of seabed.

▼ A woman harvests seaweed on a farm on the coast of Zanzibar, East Africa.

175 **Sea minerals are big business.** Minerals are useful substances that we mine from the ground – and oceans are full of them! The most valuable are oil and gas, which are pumped from the seabed and piped ashore or transported in huge supertankers. Salt is another important mineral. In hot, low-lying areas, people build walls to hold shallow pools of sea water. The water dries up in the sun, leaving behind crystals of salt.

176 **There are gemstones under the sea.** Pearls are made by oysters. If a grain of sand is lodged inside an oyster's shell, it irritates its soft body. The oyster coats the sand with a substance called nacre, which is also used to line the inside of the shell. Over the years, more nacre builds up and the pearl gets bigger.

▲ The oil platform's welded-steel legs rest on the seabed. They support the platform around 15 metres above the surface of the water.

▶ An oyster's shell must be pried open with a knife to get to the pearl inside.

QUIZ

1. What are the young of lobster called?
2. What substances are pumped from the seabed?
3. Is seaweed edible?
4. Which gemstone is made by oysters?

Answers:
1. Larvae 2. Oil and gas
3. Yes 4. Pearl

Going under

177 A submarine has dived deeper than 10,000 metres. The two-person *Trieste* made history in 1960 in an expedition to the Mariana Trench in the Pacific, the deepest part of any ocean. It took the submarine five hours to reach the bottom, a distance of 10,911 metres. On the way down, the extreme water pressure cracked part of the craft, but luckily, the two men inside returned to the surface unharmed.

▲ *Trieste* spent 20 minutes at the bottom of the Mariana Trench.

Mast to renew and expel air

Mine

Propellers

◄ The Americans used *Turtle* against the British in their War of Independence.

178 The first combat submarine was shaped like an egg! *Turtle* was a one-person submarine that made its test dive in 1776. It was the first real submarine. It did not have an engine – it was driven by a propeller turned by hand. *Turtle* was built for war. It travelled just below the surface and could fix bombs to the bottom of enemy ships.

179 Divers have a spare pair of lungs.

Scuba divers wear special breathing apparatus called 'aqua lungs'. French divers, Jacques Cousteau and Emile Gagnan, came up with the idea of a portable oxygen supply. This meant that divers were able to swim freely for the first time, rather than wearing a heavy suit and helmet.

▲ Divers control their breathing to make their oxygen supply last as long as possible.

180 The biggest submarines weighed 26,500 tonnes.

They were Russian submarines called Typhoons, built in the 1970s and 1980s. As well as being the biggest submarines, they were also the fastest, able to top 40 knots.

▼ The Typhoons did not need to come up to refuel because they were nuclear-powered.

Periscope

Rudder

Engine room

Living quarters

Torpedo firing tube

Diving plane

I DON'T BELIEVE IT!

In 1963 Jacques Cousteau built a village on the bed of the Red Sea. Along with four other divers, he lived there for a whole month.

Superboats

People said *Titanic* was unsinkable. But in 1912 it hit an iceberg and sank on its maiden voyage. More than 1500 people drowned.

181 Some ships are invisible. Stealth warships are not really invisible, of course, but they are hard to detect using radar. There are already materials being used for ships that can absorb some radar signals. Some paints can soak up radar, too, and signals are also bounced off in confusing directions by the ships' strange, angled hulls.

▶ An angled, sloping hull gives very little radar echo. This makes the stealth ship's location hard to pinpoint.

182 The biggest ship ever built was nearly half a kilometre long. It was a supertanker called *Jahre Viking*. Supertankers carry cargoes of oil around the world. They move slowly because they are so huge and heavy. *Jahre Viking* was demolished in 2009. The world's biggest ship is now a container ship called *CMA CGM Marco Polo*.

▼ The giant supertanker *Jahre Viking* was just over 458 metres long.

▼ Hovercraft can travel at up to 65 knots, the equivalent of 120 kilometres an hour.

183 Not all boats ride the waves.

Hovercrafts sit slightly above the water. They have a rubbery 'skirt' that traps a cushion of air for them to ride on. Without the drag of the water to work against, hovercraft can cross the water much faster.

▼ On an aircraft carrier, planes are constantly taking off and landing, making the flight deck a very dangerous place.

184 Ships can give piggy-backs!

Heavy-lift ships can sink part of their deck underwater, so a smaller ship can sail aboard for a free ride. Some ships carry planes. Aircraft carriers transport planes that are too small to carry enough fuel for long distances. The deck doubles up as a runway, where the planes take off and land.

▼ Some cruise ships stop at different ports during the journey, while others only stop at the beginning and end.

185 Cruise ships are floating holidays.

They are among the largest ships on the oceans today. Cruise ships usually have lots of different features, such as restaurants, shops, swimming pools, casinos, spas and bowling alleys. The biggest cruise ship in the world is currently *Allure of the Seas*, at over 360 metres in length.

Riding the waves

186 The first sea sport was surfing. It took off in the 1950s, but was invented centuries earlier in Hawaii, USA. Hawaii is still one of the best places to surf – at Waimea Bay, surfers catch waves that are up to 11 metres high. The record for the longest rides, though, are made off the coast of Mexico, where it is possible to surf for more than 1.5 kilometres.

187 A single boat towed 100 water-skiers! This record was made off the coast of Australia in 1986 and no one has beaten it yet. The drag boat was a cruiser called *Reef Cat*.

▶ Water-skiing is now one of the most popular of all water sports.

▼ Modern surfboards are made of super-light materials. This means they create little drag in the water – and the surfer can reach high speeds!

QUIZ

1. What was the name of the fastest hydroplane?
2. When did jet skis go on sale?
3. Where is Waimea Bay?
4. What is a trimaran?

Answers:
1. Spirit of Australia
2. 1973 3. Hawaii
4. A three-hulled boat

▼ Jet skis first went on sale in 1973.

189
Three hulls are sometimes better than one. Powerboating is an exciting, dangerous sport. Competitors are always trying out new boat designs that will race even faster. Multi-hulled boats minimize drag, but keep the boat steady. Trimarans have three slender, streamlined hulls that cut through the water.

188
Jet-skiers can travel at nearly 100 kilometres an hour. Jet skis were first developed in the 1960s. Their inventor was an American called Clayton Jacobsen who wanted to combine his two favourite hobbies, motorbikes and water-skiing. Today, some jet-skiers are professional sportspeople.

► Trimarans have three hulls, while catamarans have two.

▲ Hydroplanes are motor boats that skim across the surface of the water.

190
Hydroplanes fly over the waves. They are a cross between a boat and a plane. Special 'wings' raise the hull 2 metres above the water. The fastest hydroplane ever was *Spirit of Australia*. Driven by Kenneth Warby, it sped along at more than 500 kilometres an hour above the surface of the water!

Ocean stories

191 **The Greek hero Jason made an epic sea voyage.** The ancient Greeks made up lots of sea adventure stories, probably because they lived on scattered islands. In the legend of the Argonauts, a hero called Jason sets off in a boat called the Argo with a band of brave men. He goes on a quest to find the Golden Fleece, a precious sheepskin guarded by a fierce dragon.

▲ Jason and the Argonauts steer their ship between two huge moving cliffs called the Cyanean Rocks. They faced many dangers on their journey.

▼ Neptune raises his trident and whips up a storm.

192 **Neptune (or Poseidon) was an undersea god.** Poseidon was the name used by the ancient Greeks and Neptune by the ancient Romans. Both civilizations pictured their god with a fork called a trident. They blamed their gods for the terrible storms that wrecked boats in the Mediterranean.

▼ The beautiful goddess Aphrodite emerges from the sea.

195
Long ago, people believed in a giant sea monster, called the kraken. The stories were used to explain the dangers of the sea. Sightings of the giant squid might have inspired these tales.

▶ Mistaken for a monster! The 15 metre-long giant squid has eyes as big as dinner plates.

193
The Greek goddess of love was born in the sea. Aphrodite was said to be the daughter of Zeus, the king of the gods. She was born out of the foam of the sea. The Romans based their love goddess, Venus, on the same story. Lots of artists have painted her rising from the waves in a giant clam shell.

196
Mermaids lured sailors to their deaths on the rocks. Mythical mermaids were said to be half-woman, half-fish. Folklore tells how the mermaids confused sailors with their beautiful singing – with the result that their ships were wrecked on the rocks.

▼ Mermaids were said to have the tail of a fish instead of legs.

194
A mermaid's purse is the name given to the eggcases of the dog shark. They look a little bit like handbags!

WEATHER

197 Rain, sunshine, snow and storms are all types of weather. Different weather is caused by what is happening in the atmosphere – the air around and above us. In some parts of the world, the weather changes every day, but in others it is nearly always the same.

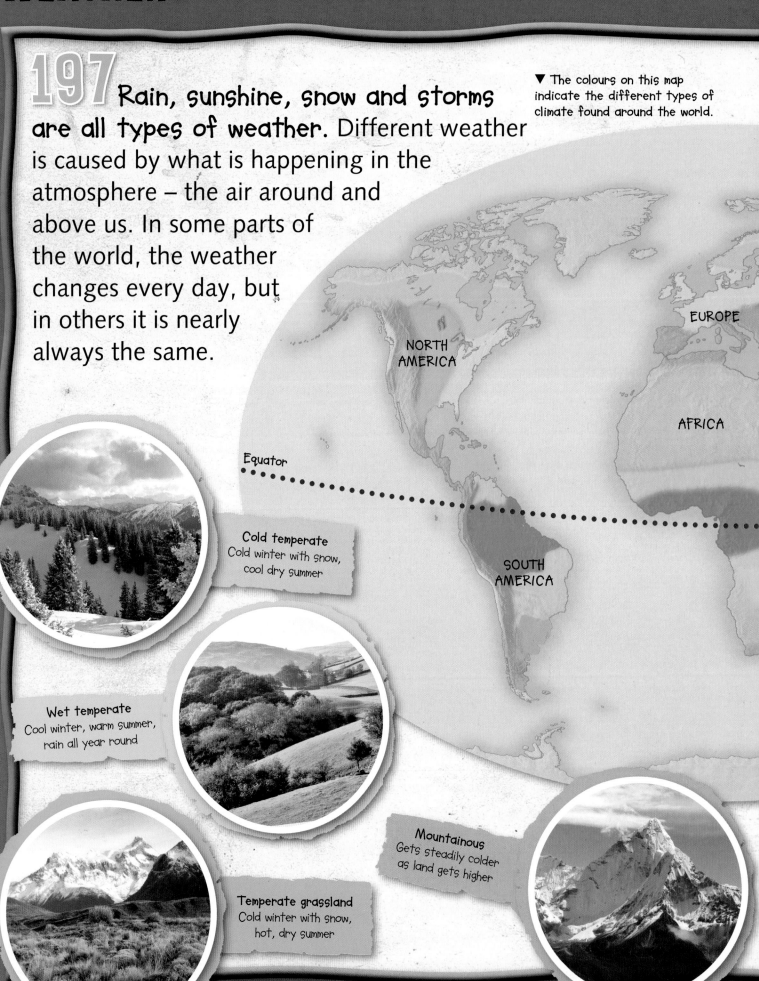

▼ The colours on this map indicate the different types of climate found around the world.

NORTH AMERICA

EUROPE

AFRICA

Equator

SOUTH AMERICA

Cold temperate
Cold winter with snow, cool dry summer

Wet temperate
Cool winter, warm summer, rain all year round

Temperate grassland
Cold winter with snow, hot, dry summer

Mountainous
Gets steadily colder as land gets higher

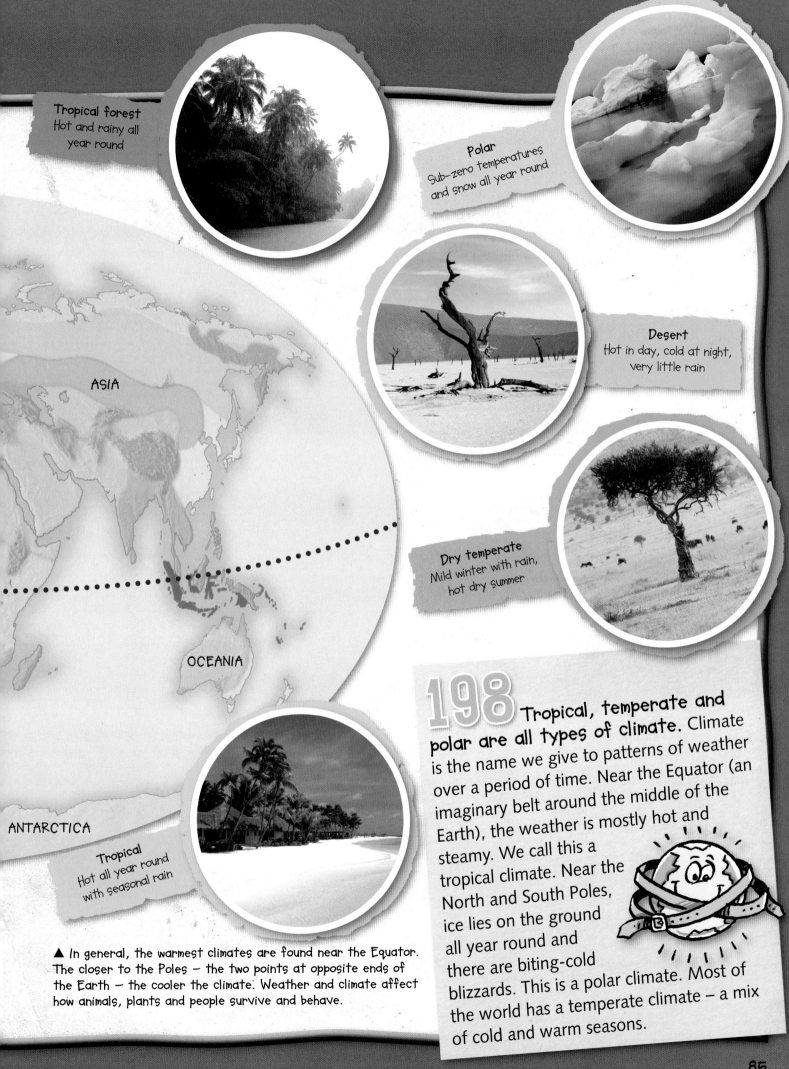

Tropical forest
Hot and rainy all year round

Polar
Sub-zero temperatures and snow all year round

Desert
Hot in day, cold at night, very little rain

Dry temperate
Mild winter with rain, hot dry summer

ASIA

OCEANIA

ANTARCTICA

Tropical
Hot all year round with seasonal rain

▲ In general, the warmest climates are found near the Equator. The closer to the Poles — the two points at opposite ends of the Earth — the cooler the climate. Weather and climate affect how animals, plants and people survive and behave.

198 Tropical, temperate and polar are all types of climate. Climate is the name we give to patterns of weather over a period of time. Near the Equator (an imaginary belt around the middle of the Earth), the weather is mostly hot and steamy. We call this a tropical climate. Near the North and South Poles, ice lies on the ground all year round and there are biting-cold blizzards. This is a polar climate. Most of the world has a temperate climate — a mix of cold and warm seasons.

Four seasons

199 **The reason we have seasons lies in space.** The pull of the Sun's gravity means Earth orbits (travels around) the Sun. One orbit takes one year to complete. Over the year, Earth's tilt causes first one and then the other Pole to lean towards the Sun, and this gives us seasons. For example, in June the North Pole is tilted towards the Sun. The Sun heats the northern half of the Earth and it is summer.

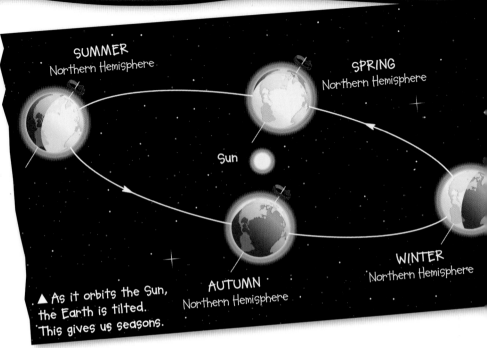

SUMMER
Northern Hemisphere

SPRING
Northern Hemisphere

Sun

WINTER
Northern Hemisphere

AUTUMN
Northern Hemisphere

▲ As it orbits the Sun, the Earth is tilted. This gives us seasons.

I DON'T BELIEVE IT!

When the Sun shines all day in the far north, there is 24-hour night in the far south.

200 **When it is summer in Argentina, it is winter in Canada.** In December, the South Pole leans towards the Sun. Places in the southern half of the world, such as Argentina, have summer. At the same time, places in the northern half, such as Canada, have winter.

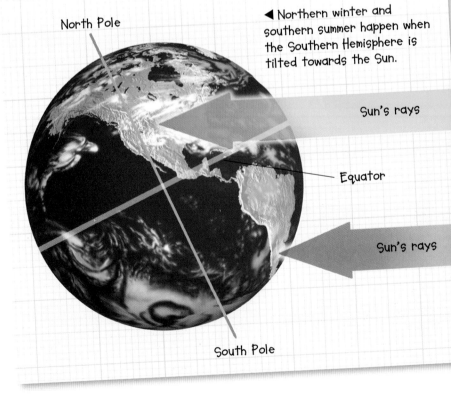

◄ Northern winter and southern summer happen when the Southern Hemisphere is tilted towards the Sun.

North Pole

Sun's rays

Equator

Sun's rays

South Pole

▼ Near the North Pole, the Sun never sets below the horizon on Midsummer's Day.

201 A day can last 21 hours!

Night and day happen because Earth is spinning as it circles the Sun. At the height of summer, places near the North Pole are so tilted towards the Sun that it is light almost all day long. In Stockholm, Sweden on Midsummer's Eve, daytime lasts for 21 hours because the Sun disappears below the horizon for only three hours.

▶ Trees that lose their leaves in autumn are called deciduous. Evergreens are trees that keep their leaves all year round.

AUTUMN

Leaves change colour and start to fall. Fruits ripen.

WINTER

Branches are bare.

SUMMER

Flowering trees are in full bloom. Some have a second growth spurt.

SPRING

Leaf buds start to grow. The leaves soon open and flowers bloom.

202 Some forests change colour in the autumn.

Autumn comes between summer and winter. Trees prepare for the cold winter months ahead by losing their leaves. First, though, they suck back the precious green chlorophyll, or dye, in their leaves, making them turn glorious shades of red, orange and brown.

87

Fewer seasons

203 Monsoons are winds that carry heavy rains. During the hot, rainy tropical summer, the Sun warms the sea, causing huge banks of cloud to form. These are blown by monsoon winds towards land. Once they hit the continent, rain can pour for weeks.

▲ When monsoon rains are especially heavy, they can cause chaos. Streets turn to rivers and sometimes people's homes are washed away.

204 Monsoons happen mainly in Asia. However, there are parts of the Americas, close to the Equator, that also have a rainy season. Winds can carry heavy rain clouds, causing flash floods in the southwestern deserts of the USA. The floods happen because the land has been baked hard during the dry season, so water doesn't drain away.

POTENTIAL FLASH FLOOD AREAS

NEXT 6 MILES

◄ This sign warns of flash flooding in California, USA.

205 Many parts of the tropics have two seasons, not four. In the parts of the world closest to the Equator it is always hot, as these places are constantly facing the Sun. However, Earth's movement affects the position of a great band of cloud. In June, the tropical areas north of the Equator have the strongest heat and the heaviest rainstorms. In December, it is the turn of the areas south of the Equator.

Tropic of Cancer

Equator

Tropic of Capricorn

▲ The tropics lie either side of the Equator, between lines of latitude called the Tropic of Cancer and the Tropic of Capricorn.

QUIZ

1. What are monsoons?
2. On which continent do most monsoons occur?
3. How many seasons are there in the tropics?
4. How much rainfall do tropical rainforests usually have in a year?

Answers:
1. Winds that carry heavy rains 2. Asia 3. Two 4. About 2000 millimetres

◄ Daily rainfall feeds lush rainforest vegetation and countless waterfalls in the mountains of Costa Rica.

206 Tropical rainforests have rainy weather all year round. There is usually about 2000 millimetres of rainfall in a year. Rainforests still have a wet and a dry season, but the wet season is even wetter! Some parts of the rainforest can become flooded during the wet season, as the heavy rain makes rivers overflow their banks.

What a scorcher!

207 **All of our heat comes from the Sun.** The Sun is a star – a ball of burning gases. The heat rays it gives off travel 150 million kilometres through space to reach Earth. The rays cool down on the journey, but are still hot enough to scorch Earth.

QUIZ

1. Where is the hottest recorded place in the world?
2. When did the 'Dust Bowl' occur?
3. What caused the 'Dust Bowl'?
4. Is El Niño a wind or a current?

Answers:
1. Death Valley in California, USA 2. The 1930s 3. Terrible drought 4. A current

208 **The Sahara is the sunniest place on Earth.** This North African desert once had 4300 hours of sunshine in a year! People who live here, such as the Tuareg Arabs, cover their skin to avoid being sunburnt.

209 **The hottest temperature on Earth was measured at Death Valley in California, USA.** An air temperature of 56.7°C was recorded in 1913. Al Aziziyah in Libya had held a record of 58°C for 90 years, but in 2012 this was reanalyzed and found to be incorrect.

◄ Desert peoples wear headdresses to protect their skin and eyes from the sun and sand.

210 **The Sun can trick your eyes.** Sometimes, as sunlight passes through our atmosphere, it hits layers of air at different temperatures. When this happens, the air bends the light and can trick our eyes into seeing something that is not there. This is a mirage. For example, what looks like a pool of water might really be part of the sky reflected on to the land.

▲ A mirage is just a trick of the light. It can make us see something that is not really there.

211 **Too much sun brings drought.** Clear skies and sunshine are not always good news. Without rain, crops wither, and people and their animals go hungry.

212 **One terrible drought made a 'Dust Bowl'.** Settlements in the American Midwest were devastated by a long drought during the 1930s. As crops died, there were no roots to hold the soil together. The dry earth turned to dust and some farms simply blew away!

▼ During the 1930s, dust storms caused by drought in Oklahoma, USA covered fields in layers of dust.

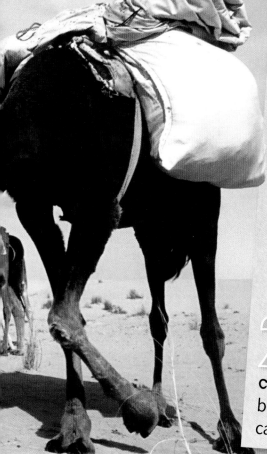

OCEANIA

Warm water

PACIFIC OCEAN

SOUTH AMERICA

Cold water

▲ El Niño has been known to cause violent weather conditions. It returns on average every four years.

213 **All sorts of things affect our weather and climate.** The movements of a sea current called El Niño have been blamed for causing flooding and terrible droughts – which can lead to unstoppable forest fires.

Our atmosphere

214 Earth is wrapped in a blanket of air called the atmosphere, which is hundreds of kilometres thick. The atmosphere keeps heat in at night, and during the day forms a sunscreen, protecting us from the Sun's fierce rays. Without it there would be no weather.

215 Most weather happens in the troposphere. This is the layer of atmosphere that stretches from the ground to around 10 kilometres above your head. The higher in the troposphere you go, the cooler the air. Because of this, clouds are most likely to form here. Clouds with flattened tops show just where the troposphere meets the next layer, the stratosphere.

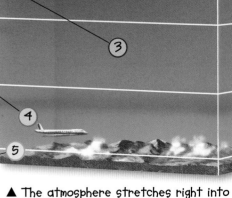

Low-level satellites orbit within the exosphere

The Northern and Southern Lights — the auroras — are formed in the thermosphere

Meteors entering the atmosphere burn up in the mesosphere, causing 'shooting stars'

Aeroplanes either fly high in the troposphere, or in the lower levels of the stratosphere

Weather forms in the troposphere

▶ This view of the Earth from the International Space Station, which orbits the Earth, shows the atmosphere as a thin, wispy layer.

▲ The atmosphere stretches right into space. Scientists have split it into five layers, or spheres.

216

Molecules (tiny particles) in the air are constantly bumping into each other. The more they do this, the greater the air pressure. There are usually more collisions lower in the troposphere, because gravity pulls the molecules towards Earth's surface. The higher you go, the lower the air pressure, and the less oxygen there is in the air.

217

Warmth makes air move. When heat from the Sun warms the molecules in air, they move faster and spread out more. This makes the air lighter, so it rises in the sky, creating low pressure. As it gets higher, the air cools. The molecules slow down and become heavier again, so they start to sink back to Earth.

HIGH PRESSURE   LOW PRESSURE

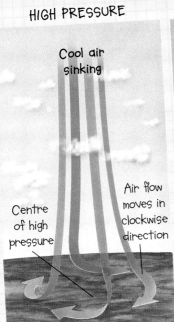

Cool air sinking

Centre of high pressure

Air flow moves in clockwise direction

Warm air rising

Centre of low pressure

Air flow moves in anticlockwise direction

▲ A high pressure weather system gives us warmer weather, while low pressure gives us cooler, more unsettled weather. (In the Northern Hemisphere, air flows anticlockwise in a low pressure system, and clockwise in high pressure. In the Southern Hemisphere, it is the opposite.)

▲ At high altitudes there is less oxygen. That is why mountaineers often wear breathing equipment.

Clouds and rain

218 Water goes on a journey called the water cycle. As the Sun heats the ocean's surface, some seawater turns to vapour and rises. As it rises, it cools and turns back into droplets, which join to make clouds. The droplets continue forming bigger drops and eventually fall as rain. Some is soaked up by land, but a lot finds its way back to the sea.

219 Some mountains are so tall that their summits are hidden by cloud. They can even affect the weather. When moving air hits a mountain slope it is forced upwards, causing its temperature to drop, and clouds to form.

▼ The peak of Chapaeva, in the Tian Shan mountain range in Asia, can be seen above the clouds.

WARM AIR

KEY

1. Water evaporates from the sea
2. Clouds form
3. Water is given off by trees
4. Rain falls, filling rivers
5. Rivers run back to the sea

▼ Water moves in a continuous cycle between the ocean, atmosphere and land.

220

Clouds release energy. When water vapour becomes water droplets and forms clouds, a small amount of heat energy is given out into the atmosphere. Then, when the droplets fall as rain, kinetic (movement) energy is released as the rain hits the ground.

RAIN GAUGE

You will need:
jam jar   waterproof marker pen
ruler   notebook   pen

Put the jar outside. At the same time each day, mark the rainwater level on the jar with your pen. At the end of a week, empty the jar. Measure and record how much rain fell each day and over the whole week.

▶ Virga happens when rain reaches a layer of dry air. The rain droplets turn back into water vapour in mid-air, and seem to disappear.

221

Some rain never reaches the ground. The raindrops turn back into water vapour because they hit a layer of super-dry air. You can actually see the drops falling like a curtain from the cloud, but the curtain stops in mid-air. This type of weather is called virga.

Not just fluffy

222 Clouds come in all shapes and sizes. Scientists divide them into three basic types according to their shape and height above the ground. Wispy cirrus clouds form high in the troposphere and rarely mean rain. Flat, layered stratus clouds may produce drizzle or a sprinkling of snow. Soft, fluffy cumulus clouds usually bring rain.

223 Cumulus humilis clouds are the smallest heap-shaped clouds. They are too small to produce rain but they can grow into much bigger, rain-carrying cumulus clouds. The biggest cumulus clouds, called cumulonimbus, bring heavy rainfall.

Cirrus
Thin, wispy high-level clouds, sometimes called 'mare's tails'

Cumulonimbus
Towering grey-white clouds that produce heavy rainfall

Cumulus
Billowing clouds with flat bases

Nimbostratus
Dense layer of low, grey rain clouds

▶ The main classes of cloud – cirrus, cumulus and stratus – were named in the 1800s. An amateur British weather scientist called Luke Howard identified the different types.

Cirrocumulus
Ripples or rows of small
white clouds at high altitude

Contrails
The white streaks
created by planes

Altocumulus
Small globular clouds
at middle altitude

224 Not all clouds are made by nature. Contrails are streaky clouds that a plane leaves behind it as it flies. They are made of water vapour that comes from the plane's engines. The second it hits the cold air, the vapour turns into ice crystals, leaving a trail of white cloud.

Altostratus
Layered grey middle-level
cloud with no visible holes

225 Sometimes the sky is filled with white patches of cloud that look like shimmering fish scales. These are called mackerel skies. It takes lots of gusty wind to break the cloud into these little patches, and so mackerel skies are usually a sign of changeable weather.

Stratocumulus
Grey clouds in patches or
globules that may join together

◄ A mackerel sky over Calanais stone circle in Scotland.

Stratus
Continuous low cloud near,
but not touching, the ground

Flood warning

226 **Too much rain brings flooding.** There are two types of floods. Flash floods happen after a short burst of heavy rain. Broadscale flooding is caused by rain falling steadily for weeks or months without stopping. Rivers fill and eventually burst their banks. Tropical storms can also lead to broadscale flooding.

227 **The ancient Egyptians had a story to explain the yearly flooding of the Nile.** They said the goddess Isis filled the river with tears, as she cried for her lost husband.

▲ The power of flood water has caused great damage to this house in Australia.

228 **There can be floods in the desert.** When a lot of rain falls very quickly on to land that has been baked dry, it cannot soak in. Instead, it sits on the surface, causing flash floods.

▼ A desert flash flood in the Grand Canyon, USA, has created streams of muddy water. After the water level falls, vegetation will burst into life.

229 The Bible tells of a terrible flood, and how a man called Noah was saved. Explorers recently found evidence of the flood – a sunken beach 140 metres below the surface of the Black Sea. There are ruins of houses, dating back to 5600 BC. Stories of a flood in ancient times do not only appear in the Bible – the Babylonians and Greeks told of one, too.

▼ In the Bible, Noah survived the Great Flood by building a huge wooden boat called an ark.

230 When rain mixes with earth it makes mud. On a mountainside, with no tree roots to hold soil together, rain can cause an avalanche of mud. In 1985 flooding in Colombia, South America, caused a terrible mudslide that buried 23,000 people from the town of Armero.

◄ Torrential rain in Brazil caused this mudslide, which swept away part of a village.

Deep freeze

▶ This truck has become stuck in a snow drift. Falling snow is made worse by strong winds, which can form deep drifts.

231 Snow is made of tiny ice crystals. At very cold air temperatures – around 0°C – water droplets in clouds freeze into tiny ice crystals. If these clump together they fall as snowflakes.

▼ A snowflake that is several centimetres across will be made up of lots of crystals, like these.

232 No two snowflakes are the same. This is because snowflakes are made up of ice crystals, and every ice crystal is as unique as your fingerprint. Most crystals look like six-pointed stars, but they come in other shapes too.

233 Black ice is not really black. Drizzle or rain turns to ice when it touches freezing-cold ground. This 'black' ice is see-through, and hard to spot against a road's dark tarmac. It is also very slippery, creating dangerous driving conditions.

I DON'T BELIEVE IT!
Antarctica is the coldest place on Earth. Temperatures of –89.2°C have been recorded there.

234

Avalanches are like giant snowballs. They can happen after lots of snow falls on a mountain. The slightest movement or sudden noise can jolt the pile of snow into moving down the slope. As it crashes down, the avalanche picks up extra snow and can end up large enough to bury whole towns.

▲ An avalanche gathers speed as it thunders down the mountainside.

235

Marksmen shoot at snowy mountains. One way to prevent deadly avalanches is to stop too much snow from building up. In mountainous areas, marksmen set off mini avalanches on purpose. They make sure people are out of the danger zone, then fire guns to trigger a snowslide.

▼ Antarctica is a frozen wilderness. The ice piles up to form amazing shapes.

236

Ice can stay frozen for millions of years. At the North and South Poles, the weather never warms up enough for the ice to thaw. When fresh snow falls, it presses down on the snow already there, forming thick sheets. Some ice may not have melted for a million years or more.

237 Wind is moving air.

Air is constantly moving from areas of high pressure to areas of low pressure. The bigger the difference in pressure between the two areas, the faster the wind blows.

▶ In open, exposed areas, trees can be forced into strange shapes by the wind.

238 World wind patterns are called global winds.

The most famous are the trade winds that blow towards the Equator. Well-known local winds include the cold, dry mistral that blows down to southern France, and the hot, dry sirroco that blows north of the Sahara.

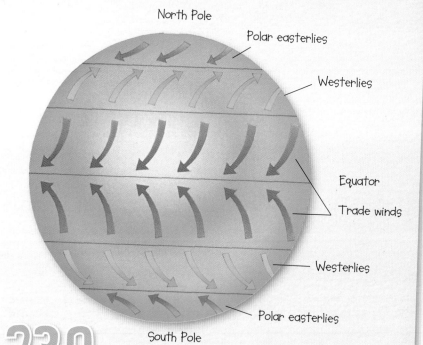

▼ This map shows the pattern of the world's main winds.

North Pole

Polar easterlies

Westerlies

Equator

Trade winds

Westerlies

Polar easterlies

South Pole

239 Trade winds blow from east to west, above and below the Equator.

In the tropics, air is moving to an area of low pressure at the Equator. The winds blow towards the Equator, from the southeast in the Southern Hemisphere, and the northeast in the Northern Hemisphere. Their name comes from their importance to traders, when goods travelled across the oceans by sailing ship.

240 You can tell how windy it is by looking at the leaves on a tree. Wind strength is measured on the Beaufort Scale, named after the Irish admiral who devised it. Based on the visible effects of wind, the scale ranges from Force 0 – total calm, to Force 12 – hurricane.

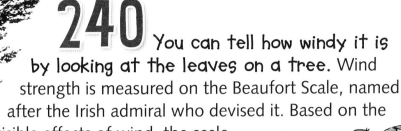

241 Wind can bring very changeable weather. The Föhn wind, which blows across Switzerland, Austria and Bavaria in southern Germany, brings rapid rises in temperature, sometimes by as much as 30°C in a matter of hours. It has been blamed for various illnesses, including bouts of madness!

242 Wind can turn on your TV. People can harness the energy of wind to make electricity for our homes. Tall turbines are positioned in windy places. As the wind turns the turbine, the movement powers a generator and produces electrical energy.

▼ Wind energy doesn't create any harmful pollution, and it will never run out.

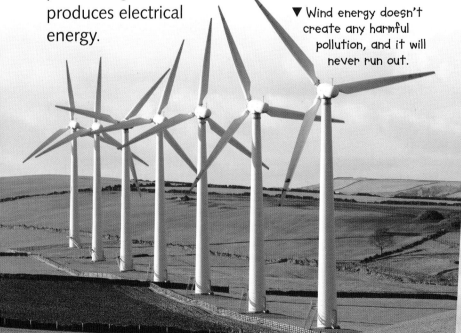

The Beaufort Scale

Force 0: Calm
Smoke rises straight up

Force 1: Light air
Wind motion visible in smoke

Force 2: Light breeze
Leaves rustle

Force 3: Gentle breeze
Twigs move, light flags flap

Force 4: Moderate breeze
Small branches move

Force 5: Fresh breeze
Bushes and small trees sway

Force 6: Strong breeze
Large branches in motion

Force 7: Near gale
Whole trees sway

Force 8: Gale
Difficult to walk or move, twigs break

Force 9: Strong gale
Tiles and chimneys may be blown from rooftops

Force 10: Storm
Trees uprooted

Force 11: Violent storm
Widespread damage to buildings

Force 12: Hurricane
Severe devastation

Thunderbolts and lightning

243 **Thunderstorms are most likely to occur in summer.** Warm, moist air rises and forms cumulonimbus clouds. Inside the clouds, water droplets and ice crystals move about, building up positive and negative electrical charges. Electricity flows between the charges, creating a flash (lightning). The air heated by the lightning expands, causing a loud noise, or thunderclap.

▼ Cloud-to-cloud lightning is called sheet lightning. Lightning travelling from the cloud to the ground, as shown here, is called fork lightning.

HOW CLOSE?

Lightning and thunder happen at the same time, but light travels faster than sound. Count the seconds between the flash and the clap and divide them by three. This is how many kilometres away the storm is.

▼ Dramatic lightning flashes in Arizona, USA, light up the sky.

244 **Lightning comes in different colours.** If there is rain in the thundercloud, the lightning looks red or pink, and if there's hail, it looks blue. Lightning can also be yellow or white.

▼ Hailstones can be huge! These ones are as big as a golf ball.

245 Chunks of ice called hailstones can fall from thunderclouds. The biggest hailstones fell in Gopaljang, Bangladesh, in 1986 and weighed one kilogram each!

246 A person can survive a lightning strike. Lightning is very dangerous and can give a big enough electric shock to kill you. However, an American park ranger called Roy Sullivan survived being struck seven times.

247 Tall buildings are protected from lightning. Church steeples and other tall structures are often struck by bolts of lightning. This could damage the building, or give electric shocks to people inside, so lightning conductors are placed on the roof. These channel the lightning safely away.

◄ If lightning hits a conductor it is carried safely to the ground.

Eye of the hurricane

248 Wind speeds may reach more than 120 kilometres an hour. Violent tropical storms occur when strong winds blow into an area of low pressure and start to spin. They develop over warm seas, getting faster until they hit land, and there is no more moist sea air to feed them.

249 The centre of a hurricane is calm and still. This part is called the 'eye'. As the eye of the storm passes over, there is a pause in the terrifying rain and wind.

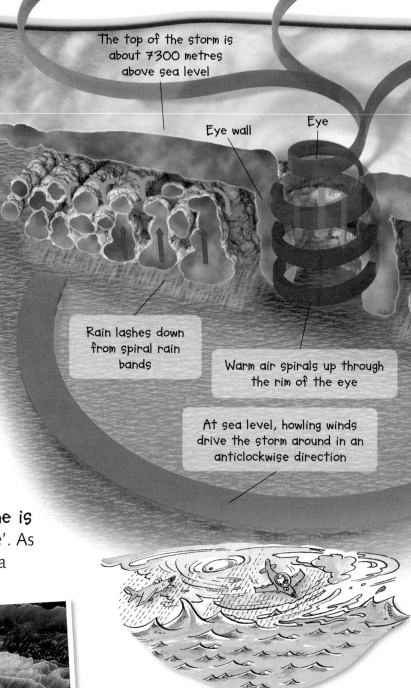

The top of the storm is about 7300 metres above sea level

Eye wall

Eye

Rain lashes down from spiral rain bands

Warm air spirals up through the rim of the eye

At sea level, howling winds drive the storm around in an anticlockwise direction

▲ This satellite photograph shows how the storm whirls around the central, still 'eye' of the hurricane.

250 Hurricane Hunters fly close to the eye of a hurricane. These are special weather planes that fly into the storm in order to take measurements such as atmospheric pressure. It is a dangerous job for the pilots, but the information they gather helps to predict the hurricane's path – and saves lives.

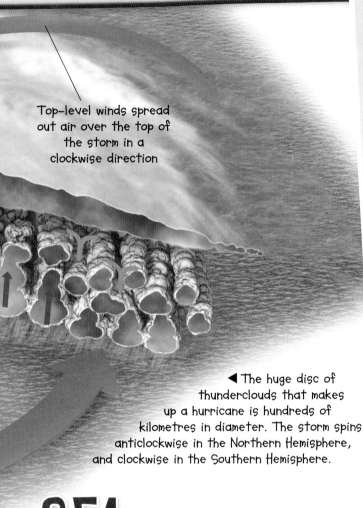

Top-level winds spread out air over the top of the storm in a clockwise direction

◄ The huge disc of thunderclouds that makes up a hurricane is hundreds of kilometres in diameter. The storm spins anticlockwise in the Northern Hemisphere, and clockwise in the Southern Hemisphere.

252 Hurricanes make the sea rise.

As the storm races over the ocean, its strong winds push on the seawater in front of it. This causes seawater to pile up, sometimes more than 10 metres high, which hits the shore as a storm surge. In 1961, the storm surge following Hurricane Hattie washed away Belize City in South America.

▼ Massive waves crash onto shore in Rhode Island, USA, during Superstorm Sandy in October 2012. Sandy began as a hurricane, but was downgraded to a storm.

251 Hurricanes have names.

The National Weather Service in the USA officially began a naming system in 1954. One of the worst hurricanes was Hurricane Katrina, which battered the US coast from Florida to Texas in August 2005.

253 Typhoons saved the Japanese from Genghis Khan.

The 13th-century Mongol leader made two attempts to invade Japan – and both times, a terrible typhoon battered his fleet of ships and saved the Japanese!

◄ A typhoon prevented Genghis Khan's navy from invading Japan.

Twisting tornadoes

254 Tornadoes are among the most destructive storms. Also known as twisters, these whirling columns of wind form in strong thunderstorms. When the back part of the thundercloud starts spinning, the spinning air forms a funnel that reaches down towards the ground. As it touches the ground, it becomes a tornado.

255 A spinning tornado whizzes along the ground, sucking up everything in its path. It may rip the roofs off houses, and even toss whole buildings into the air. In the 1930s, a twister in Minnesota, USA, threw a train carriage full of people over 8 metres into the air!

▶ A tornado can cause great damage to anything in its path, reaching speeds of up to 480 kilometres an hour.

I DON'T BELIEVE IT!

Loch Ness in Scotland is famous for sightings of a monster nicknamed Nessie. Perhaps people who have seen Nessie were really seeing a waterspout.

▶ The shaded area shows Tornado Alley, where there are hundreds of tornadoes each year.

USA

Minneapolis

Sioux Falls

Chicago

Denver

Kansas City

Wichita

St Louis

Amarillo

Oklahoma City

Dallas

New Orleans

Houston

MEXICO

256 Tornado Alley is a twister hotspot in the American Midwest. This is where hot air travelling north from the Gulf of Mexico meets cold polar winds travelling south, and creates huge thunderclouds. Of course, tornadoes can happen anywhere in the world when the conditions are right.

257 A pillar of whirling water can rise out of a lake or the sea. Waterspouts are spiralling columns of water that can be sucked up by a tornado as it forms over a lake or the sea. They tend to spin more slowly than tornadoes because water is much heavier than air.

◀ Waterspouts can suck up fish from a lake!

258 Dust devils are similar to tornadoes, and form in deserts and other dry dusty areas. They shift tonnes of sand and can cause terrible damage – stripping the paintwork from a car in seconds.

◀ A desert dust devil in Amboseli National Park, Kenya.

Sky lights

259 **Rainbows are caused by sunlight passing through raindrops.** The water acts like a glass prism, splitting the light. White light is made up of seven colours – red, orange, yellow, green, blue, indigo and violet. These colours, from top to bottom, make up the rainbow.

260 **Halos can form around the Sun or Moon!** If you look at the Sun or Moon through clouds containing tiny ice crystals, they seem to be surrounded by a glowing ring of light.

◀ Rainbows are often seen after rain has stopped.

261 **Two rainbows can appear at once.** This is caused by the light being reflected twice inside a raindrop. The top rainbow is a reflection of the bottom one, so its colours appear the opposite way round, with the violet band at the top and red at the bottom.

262 **Some rainbows appear at night.** They happen when falling raindrops split moonlight, rather than sunlight. This sort of rainbow is called a moonbow. They are very rare, and can only be seen in a few places in the world.

◀ A halo around the Sun or Moon can be a sign that a storm is coming.

263 **A rainbow's colours always appear in the same order:** (from top to bottom) red, orange, yellow, green, blue, indigo, violet. The first letter of each word in this sentence gives the first letter of each colour in order: Richard Of York Gave Battle In Vain.

▼ Mock suns are also known as parhelia or sundogs.

▼ An aurora – the most dazzling natural light show on Earth!

264 **Three suns can appear in the sky.** 'Mock suns' are two bright spots that appear on either side of the Sun. They often happen at the same time as a halo, and have the same cause – light passing through ice crystals in the air.

265 **Auroras are curtains of lights in the sky.** They happen in the far north and south of the world when particles from the Sun smash into molecules in the air – at speeds of 1600 kilometres an hour. The lights may be blue, red, yellow or green.

▼ Although a fogbow is colourless, its inner edge may appear slightly blue and its outer edge slightly red.

266 **Some rainbows are just white.** Fogbows happen when sunlight passes through a patch of fog. The water droplets in the fog are too small to work like prisms, so the arching bow is white or colourless.

Animal survival

267 Camels can go for two weeks without a drink. They are adapted to life in a hot, dry climate. Camels do not sweat until their body temperature hits 40°C, which helps them to save water. Their humps are fat stores, which are used for energy when food and water is scarce.

◄ Many desert creatures, such as this gecko, come out at night when it is cooler.

268 Lizards lose salt through their noses. Most animals get rid of excess salt in their urine, but lizards, such as iguanas and geckos, live in dry parts of the world. They need to lose as little water from their bodies as possible.

▲ Being able to withstand long periods without water means that camels can survive in the harsh desert environment.

269 Even toads can survive in the desert. The spadefoot toad copes with desert conditions by staying underground in a burrow for most of the year. It only comes to the surface after a shower of rain.

◄ Beneath its gleaming-white fur, the polar bear's skin is black to absorb heat from the Sun.

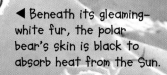

1. What is inside a camel's hump?
2. When do spadefoot toads come out of their burrows?
3. What helps to keep polar bears warm?
4. How do lizards lose excess salt from their bodies?

Answers:
1. Fat stores 2. After rain
3. Their body fat and thick fur
4. Through their noses

270 **Polar bears have black skin.** These bears have all sorts of special ways to survive the polar climate. Plenty of body fat and thick fur keeps them snug and warm, while their black skin soaks up as much warmth from the Sun as possible.

271 **Acorn woodpeckers store nuts for winter.** Animals in temperate climates have to be prepared if they are to survive the cold winter months. Acorn woodpeckers turn tree trunks into larders. During autumn, when acorns are ripe, the birds collect as many as they can, storing them in holes that they bore into a tree.

◄ Storing acorns for food helps this woodpecker survive the cold winter months.

Myths and legends

272 **People once believed the Sun was a god.** The sun god was often the most important god of all, bringing light and warmth and ripening crops. Ra, the ancient Egyptian sun god, was head of a group of nine gods. The Aztecs believed that their sun god, Huitzilpochtli, had shown them where to build their capital.

273 **Hurricanes are named after a god.** The Mayan people lived in Central America, the part of the world that is most affected by hurricanes. Their creator god was called Huracan.

▼ Viking myths tell how Thor was killed in a great battle by a giant serpent.

▲ The Egyptian sun god Ra was often shown with the head of a falcon.

274 **The Vikings thought a god brought thunder.** Thor was the god of war and thunder, worshipped across what is now Scandinavia. The Vikings pictured Thor as a red-bearded giant. He carried a hammer that produced bolts of lightning. Our day, Thursday, is named in Thor's honour.

275 **People once danced for rain.** In hot places such as Africa, people developed dances in the hope that they would bring rain. These were performed by the village shaman (a person thought to have a strong connection to spirits), using wooden instruments such as bullroarers. Sometimes water was sprinkled on the ground. Rain dances are still performed in some countries today.

276 **Totem poles honoured the Thunderbird.** Certain tribes of Native American Indians built tall, painted totem poles, carved in the image of the Thunderbird. They wanted to keep the spirit happy, because they thought it brought rain to feed the plants.

▶ A Native American Indian totem pole depicting the spirit of the Thunderbird.

MAKE A BULLROARER

You will need:
wooden ruler   string

Ask an adult to drill a hole in one end of the ruler. Thread through the string, and knot it, to stop it slipping through the hole. In an open space, whirl the instrument above your head to create a wind noise!

◀ A Mexican rain-dancer in traditional Mayan costume.

Weather folklore

277 'Red sky at night, shepherd's delight' is one of the most famous pieces of weather lore. In regions where weather systems come mostly from the west, a dramatic red sunset usually means fair weather is on its way, as a red sky is caused by high pressure. The saying is also known as 'sailor's delight'.

▼ A beautiful sunset could help a sailor to predict the next day's weather.

278 People used to say that cows lie down when rain is coming — but there is no truth in it! They lie down whether rain is on the way or not!

279 Seaweed can tell us if rain is on the way. Long ago, people looked to nature for clues about the weather. One traditional way of forecasting was to hang up strands of seaweed. If the seaweed stayed slimy, the air was damp and rain was likely. If the seaweed shrivelled up, the weather would be dry.

280

'Clear moon, frost soon'. This old saying does have some truth in it. If there are few clouds in the sky, the view of the Moon will be clear – and there will also be no blanket of cloud to keep in the Earth's heat. That makes a frost more likely – during the colder months, at least.

▶ The Moon is clearly visible when there are few clouds in the night sky. Its light casts a silvery glow over the Earth.

◀ Early Chinese weather-watchers recorded their observations on pieces of tortoiseshell.

281

The earliest weather records are over 3000 years old. They were found on a piece of tortoiseshell and had been written by Chinese weather-watchers. The inscriptions describe when it rained or snowed and how windy it was.

▶ Groundhogs emerge from their underground homes in spring following their winter hibernation.

282

Groundhogs tell the weather when they wake. In parts of the USA, Groundhog Day is a huge celebration. On 2 February, people gather to see the groundhog come out of its burrow. If it is cloudy and the groundhog has a shadow, it means there are six more weeks of cold to come. There is no evidence that this is true, though.

Instruments and inventors

▼ This is how the Tower of Winds looks today.

283 The Tower of Winds is the first known weather station. It was built by Andronicus of Cyrrhus in Athens, Greece around 75 BC. It had a wind vane on the roof and a water clock inside. Its eight sides were built to face the points of the compass.

284 The first barometer was made by one of Galileo's students. Barometers measure air pressure. The first person to describe and make an instrument for measuring air pressure was an Italian called Evangelista Torricelli (1608–1647). He had studied under the great scientist Galileo. Torricelli made his barometer in 1643.

◄ Torricelli took a bowl of mercury and placed it under the open end of a glass tube, also filled with mercury. It was the pressure of air on the mercury in the bowl that stopped the mercury in the tube from falling.

285 Weather vanes have been used since around 50 BC. They are placed on the highest point of a building, and have four fixed pointers to show north, south, east and west. A shape on the top swivels freely, so when the wind blows it points in the direction that the wind is blowing from.

286

A weather house really can predict the weather. It is a type of hygrometer – an instrument that detects how much moisture is in the air. If there is lots, the rainy-day character comes out of the door!

◄ Weather houses have two figures. One comes out when the air is damp, and the other when the air is dry.

▲ This early thermometer shows both the Fahrenheit and the Celsius temperature scales.

287

Fahrenheit made the first thermometer in 1714. Thermometers are instruments that measure temperature. Gabriel Daniel Fahrenheit (1686–1736) invented the thermometer using a blob of mercury sealed in an airtight tube. The Fahrenheit scale for measuring heat was named after him. The Centigrade scale was introduced in 1742 by the Swedish scientist Anders Celsius (1701–1744).

► Anders Celsius came from a family of scientists and astronomers.

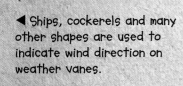

◄ Ships, cockerels and many other shapes are used to indicate wind direction on weather vanes.

What's the forecast?

288 Predicting the weather is called forecasting. Forecasters study the atmosphere and look at weather patterns. They then use computers to work out what the weather will be like over the coming days.

 A cold front is shown by a blue triangle

 A warm front is shown by a red semi-circle

 Black lines with red semi-circles and blue triangles show where a cold front meets a warm front

 White lines called isobars connect places of equal air pressure

 This symbol shows wind strength and direction. The circle shows how much cloud cover there is

 This symbol shows that the wind is very strong – look at the three lines on the tail

 This shows an area of calm, with some cloud cover

▲ Meteorologists call their weather maps synoptic charts. The symbols they use make up a common language for weather scientists all around the world.

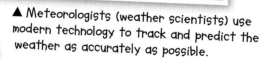

▲ Meteorologists (weather scientists) use modern technology to track and predict the weather as accurately as possible.

WEATHER SYMBOLS

Learn how to represent the weather on your own synoptic charts. Here are some of the basic symbols to get you started. You may come across them in newspapers or while watching television. Can you guess what they mean?

289 Nations need to share weather data. By 1865, nearly 60 weather stations across Europe were swapping information. These early meteorologists realized that they needed to present their data using symbols that they could all understand. Today, meteorologists still plot their data on maps called synoptic charts. Lines called isobars link areas of the same air pressure. Symbols indicate temperature and wind.

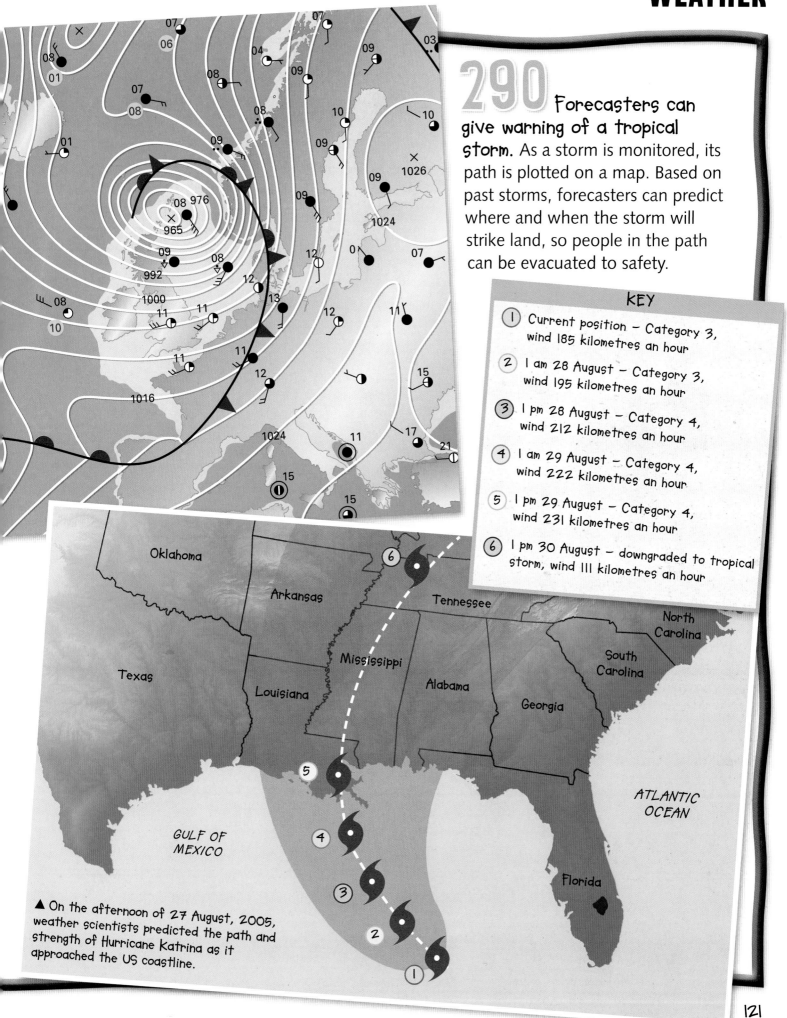

290 **Forecasters can give warning of a tropical storm.** As a storm is monitored, its path is plotted on a map. Based on past storms, forecasters can predict where and when the storm will strike land, so people in the path can be evacuated to safety.

KEY

① Current position – Category 3, wind 185 kilometres an hour

② 1 am 28 August – Category 3, wind 195 kilometres an hour

③ 1 pm 28 August – Category 4, wind 212 kilometres an hour

④ 1 am 29 August – Category 4, wind 222 kilometres an hour

⑤ 1 pm 29 August – Category 4, wind 231 kilometres an hour

⑥ 1 pm 30 August – downgraded to tropical storm, wind 111 kilometres an hour

▲ On the afternoon of 27 August, 2005, weather scientists predicted the path and strength of Hurricane Katrina as it approached the US coastline.

Weather watch

291 Weather balloons carry instruments into the atmosphere. They are filled with helium, which is lighter than air, causing the balloon to rise to a height of almost 30 kilometres. Instruments attached to the balloon measure the temperature, pressure and moisture content of the air, and send the information back to meteorologists on the ground. By tracking a balloon's position, they can also measure the speed and direction of high-altitude winds.

▲ NASA's DC-8 plane is a flying laboratory that gathers vital information about different types of weather.

293 Some planes hound the weather. Weather planes provide more detailed information about the atmosphere than balloons can. They can monitor changes in the atmosphere, and detect air pollution. They can also gather information about what causes different types of weather, and help to improve forecasting.

▶ Hundreds of weather balloons around the world are launched every day. This one is being launched into a thunderstorm by a group of weather researchers.

292 Astronauts can take incredible weather photos from space. From far above Earth, they have a great view of weather activity such as storms and aurorae.

294
Weather satellites provide vital information. Their cameras can spot the spiralling cloud pattern of a tropical storm while it is still mid-ocean, helping forecasters to issue warnings in good time. Heat-sensitive infra-red cameras measure cloud temperature, and are important in forecasting snowfall. Satellite-based radar can also measure the thickness of cloud cover, and the height of ocean waves.

▲ A weather satellite takes photographs of Earth's weather systems from space.

▲ A satellite photo showing two spiral weather systems in the North Atlantic Ocean.

▶ Weather information is collected from even the remotest parts of the globe. This weather monitoring station is inside the Arctic Circle.

295
Ground-based weather radar that can detect rainfall and wind speed is used at airports. Knowledge of the exact weather conditions is critical for pilots during take-off and landing. Weather radar is also used to track the formation and path of tornadoes, and at sea, radar can give warning of icebergs.

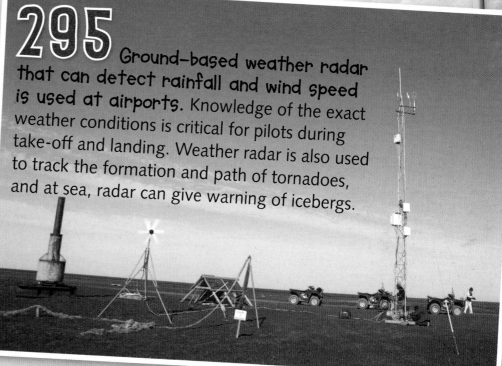

Changing climate

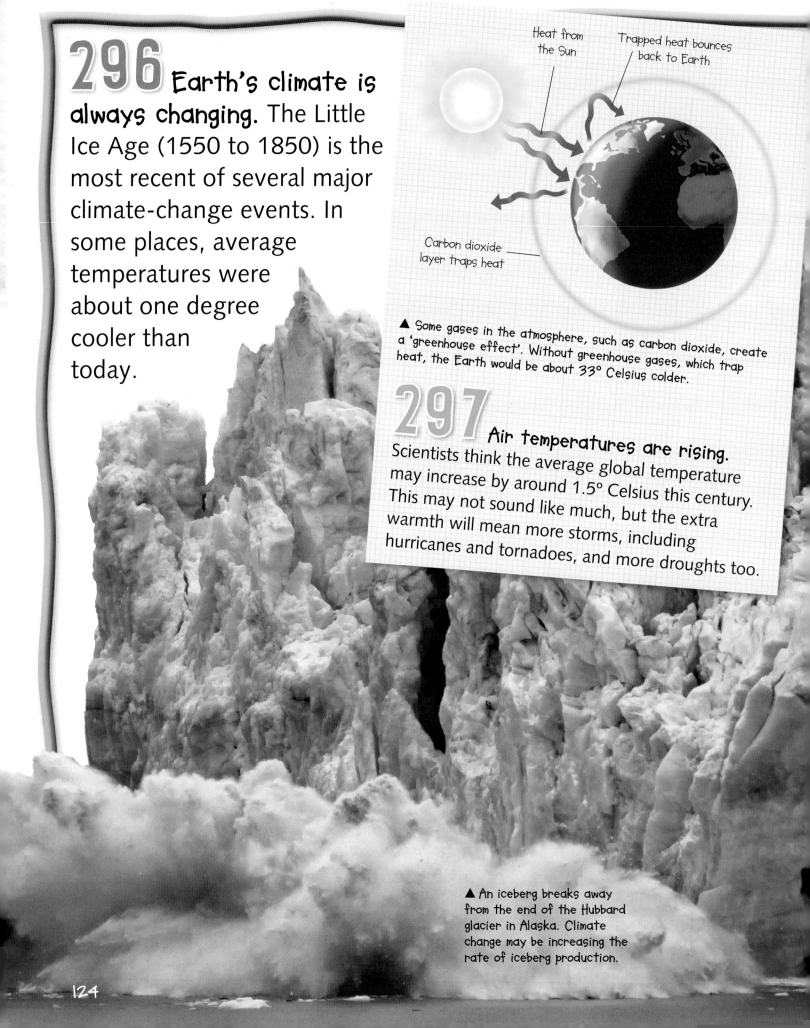

296 Earth's climate is always changing. The Little Ice Age (1550 to 1850) is the most recent of several major climate-change events. In some places, average temperatures were about one degree cooler than today.

Heat from the Sun

Trapped heat bounces back to Earth

Carbon dioxide layer traps heat

▲ Some gases in the atmosphere, such as carbon dioxide, create a 'greenhouse effect'. Without greenhouse gases, which trap heat, the Earth would be about 33° Celsius colder.

297 Air temperatures are rising. Scientists think the average global temperature may increase by around 1.5° Celsius this century. This may not sound like much, but the extra warmth will mean more storms, including hurricanes and tornadoes, and more droughts too.

▲ An iceberg breaks away from the end of the Hubbard glacier in Alaska. Climate change may be increasing the rate of iceberg production.

298 Tree-felling is affecting our weather.
In areas of Southeast Asia and South America, rainforests are being cleared for farming. When the trees are burned, the fires release carbon dioxide – a greenhouse gas that helps to blanket the Earth and keep in the heat. High levels of carbon dioxide raise the temperature too much.

▶ Like all plants, rainforest trees take in carbon dioxide and give out oxygen. As rainforests are destroyed, the amount of carbon dioxide in the atmosphere increases.

299 Some sea creatures, such as the colourful corals that live mainly in shallow water, are very sensitive to temperature.
As the atmosphere gradually warms up, so does the temperature of the surface water. This causes the coral animals, called polyps, to die, leaving behind their lifeless, stony skeletons.

◀ The death of corals through changes in water temperature is known as 'bleaching'.

QUIZ
1. When was the Little Ice Age?
2. Where do corals mainly live?
3. What gas is released when trees are burned?

Answers:
1. 1550 to 1850 2. In shallow water 3. Carbon dioxide

300 The long-term effects of climate change are uncertain.
In the short-term it seems very likely that the climate will become more unstable, and that there will be an increase in the number and intensity of extreme weather events. Weather forecasting has always been important, but in the future it will become even more so as we adapt to Earth's changing climate.

Index

Entries in **bold** refer to main subject entries. Entries in *italics* refer to illustrations

ACKNOWLEDGEMENTS

The publishers would like to thank the following sources for the use of their photographs:

Key: t = top, b = bottom, l = left, r = right, c = centre, bg = background

Cover (front) Mark Garlick/Science Photo Library

Corbis 15 Douglas Peebles; 18(t) Craig Tuttle; 21(m) Jeff Vanuga; 28(m) Lloyd Cluff; 32(tr) Michael S. Yamashita; 93 Robert Holmes; 120(l) Michele Eve Sandberg; 122–123 Jim Reed/Science Faction

Dreamstime.com 23(tr) Mirkamoksha; 63(bl) Biolifepics; 70(m) Bluesunphoto; 78(c) Perstock; 79(cr) Bladerunner88; 81(cr) Expozer; 107(t) Wickedgood; 111(c), (b) Astrofireball; 125(b) Naluphoto

FLPA 36(m) Phil McLean; 37(t) Michael & Patricia Fogden/Minden Pictures; 64(t) Tui De Roy/Minden Pictures; 67(c) Norbert Wu/Minden Pictures; 95(b) Yva Momatiuk & John Eastcott/Minden Pictures

Fotolia.com paper (throughout) Konstantin Sutyagin, Anette Linnea Rasmus; graph paper (throughout) Sharpshot; 25(t) (blue paper) Alexey Khromushin; 36(c) (yellow paper) U.P.images; 74(c) (paper) pdtnc; 86(b) Sharpshot

Glow Images 91(c) Science Faction

iStockphoto.com Cover (back, second from t) janrysavy; 16(m) Lukáš Hejtman; 23(m) IMPALASTOCK; 26(m) weareadventurers; 49(b) Joshua Haviv; 74(b) brytta; 84(bl) David Mathies; 87(t) alohaspirit; 111(t) Scene_It; 112(m) Sean Randall; 125(t) luoman

NASA 9(tr); 92(bl) NASA/JPL/UCSD/JSC; 122(t) NASA/Lori Losey; 123(tl) Jesse Allen, Earth Observatory

Naturepl.com 65(r) Jurgen Freund; 66(t) David; Shale; 68(m) Doug Perrine

Rex Features 99(m); KeystoneUSA-ZUMA

Science Photo Library 94–95(m) Gary Hincks

Shutterstock.com Cover (back, tr) beboy, (back, third from t) Christy Nicholas, (back, br) Todd Shoemake, (back, c) kornilov007, (back, bl) urosr; 1 (tl to br) Vadim Petrakov, haveseen, Lee Prince, douglas knight, agrosse, PhotoHouse; 2–3 Richard Cavalleri; 4–5 (t) rayjunk; 5(inset 1), (inset 2) sl_photo, (inset 3) Creative Travel Projects; 10–11 Alexey Repka; 11(bl) Wild Arctic Pictures, (cr) Snowbelle;

13(b) Sam DCruz; 18(b) Jose Gil; 19(m) Jarno Gonzalez Zarraonandia; 20(m) Becky Stares; 24(b) yvon52; 25(c) urosr, (b) Crepesoles; 29(tl) Menna, (tc) Spirit of America, (tr) yankane; 31(tr) MarcelClemens, (br) douglas knight; 32(l) Denis Selivanov; 35(t) Oliver Klimek; 37(b) Steve Bower; 38(b) Vadim Petrakov, 39(b) Willem Tims; 41(l) Rich Carey, 42(t) Krzysztof Odziomek, (b) Cathy Keifer; 46–47(m) ktsdesign, (bg) Aubrey Laughlin; 51(t) fashcool, (b) Regien Paassen; 54(tr) agrosse; 56–57(t) Boris Pamikov; 56(br) cynoclub; 57(b) Lynsey Allan; 59(b) Ian Scott; 60–61 powell'sPoint; 60(b) Eric Isselee; 61(t) Luna Vandoorne; 62–63 Mariusz; 62(l) worldswildlifewonders; 63(t) Vladimir Melnik; 64(b) Andrea Ricordi; 68(b) Arto Hakola, 69(m) foryouinf, (t) AridOcean; 70(br) Mariko Yuki; 71(t) Gail Johnson, (bl) Jenny Leonard; 73(br) BMJ; 74(t) DJTaylor; 72–73 Rich Lindie; 72(t) steve estvanik; 80(m) Jeanne Provost, (b) CLChang; 81(t) Kevin Eaves, (br) Asaf Eliason; (b) Darren 77(t) JonMilnes; 79(t) Dave Turner, (b) Ruth Peterkin; 80(m) Jeanne Brode; 84(tl) Seriousjoy, (c) Wild Arctic Pictures, (c) Pichugin Dmitry, (br) Oleg 85(tl) haveseen, (bl) Tatiana Popova, (b) Mark Sayer; 86(t) Redsapphire; 88(m) 1000 Words, Znamenskiy, (tr) Morozova Oxana, (b) Mark Sayer; 86(t) Redsapphire; 89(b) Dmitriy Bryndin; 90–91(m) Roca; 91(t) Loskutnikov; 94(b) Alexandr Zyryanov; (tr) Morozova Oxana, (b) Mark Sayer; 86(t) Redsapphire; 89(b) Mike Buchheit; 97(b) Christy Nicholas; 98(t) Olivier Le Queinec, (b) Mikhail Pogosov, 100(m) Bull's-Eye Arts; 101(tl) Brandelet, (tr) Mikhail Pogosov, (b) Armin Rose; 102(t) cam; 103(bl) Stephen Meese, (Force 4) Vlue, Spinu, (Force 1) Sinelyov, (Force 2) Jennifer Griner, (Force 7) photobank.kiev. (Force 5) Martin Preston, (Force 6) behindlens, (Force 10) ua, (Force 8) Robert Hoetink, (Force 9) Slobodan Djajic, (Force 10) Ortodox, (Force 11) Dustie, (Force 12) MelissaBrandes; 104–105 kornilov007; 105(bl) Sam DCruz, (c) Gunnar Pippel, (tl) Jack Dagley Photography; 109(bl) DarkOne, (br) javarman; 110(m) PhotoHouse, (bl) pzAxe; 112(t) EcoPrint; 113(t) outdoorsman, (b) Jean-Edouard Rozey; 115(l) Patryk Kosmider, (r) riekephotos; 116(m) AdamEdwards; 117(t) photomaster, (b) Squarciomomo; 118(t) Khirman Vladimir; 118–119(b) Steve Mann; 119(c) AISPIX by Image Source; 121(b) Map Resources; 123(r) George Burba; 124(m) Lee Prince

Wikimedia commons 119(b) Olof Arenius

All other photographs are from: digitalSTOCK, digitalvision, ImageState, iStockphoto.com, John Foxx, PhotoAlto, PhotoDisc, PhotoEssentials, PhotoPro, Stockbyte

Every effort has been made to acknowledge the source and copyright holder of each picture. Miles Kelly Publishing apologizes for any unintentional errors or omissions.